According to Leisha...According to God

*A true story of how tragedy and brokenness
are met with the grace and healing touch of God*

Wanda Labbe

According to Leisha, According to God
Kindle Direct Publishing
https://kdp.amazon.com

According to Leisha, According to God
Smashwords
Los Gatos, CA 95032
https://www.smashwords.com

ISBN 978-1-797-80938-0
ISBN 978-0-692-97694-4
ISBN 978-0-692-97693-7

Library of Congress Control Number 2017917755

Printed in the United States of America
10 9 8 7 6 5 4 3 2 1

Dedication

Dedicated to my beautiful, Leisha, who brought joy, fulfillment and love to all our hearts. You filled all our lives with sunshine and warmth. Someday we'll be together again, this time forever with no goodbyes.

Contents

Introduction

When tragedy strikes, are we ever prepared? Like millions of people, I occasionally thought about the terrible things that could come my way. But also like millions of others, I thought those things would never find their way into *my* life...they happened to *other* people. Nevertheless, I processed various scenarios in my head, planning what actions I might put into place just in case. With only a small obstacle here and there, things went smoothly most of the time. Then one random day that momentum changed. One major challenge after another began falling into my path. Blow after blow, I took the punches but stood strong. After shaking off the impact of each, I'd look for the bright side and begin plowing forward with the normal optimism and determination that had always driven my life. Waiting in line, though, was a much bigger opponent...the death of my daughter. Before I could prepare, it hit hard with no reservation or sympathy. All I had believed in was instantly destroyed. Though sur- rounded by family and friends I felt completely alone. Even a God I had trusted in suddenly seemed non-existent. How could He let this happen?!

I'd grown up in a large family and had a very happy childhood. When I had children, I wanted to provide that same sense of security, values and experiences my parents had given me. As time passed, we developed trust, traditions and respect for each other. Like most families, we shared good times and bad. We had plans and dreams for our future. Everything was happy…everything was on track. That happiness was abruptly halted when Leisha's life ended. I had not, nor could I ever have been, prepared for this type of tragedy. Nothing was logical or minuscule about it. When this level of grief hits, you don't just pick up the pieces the next day and move on. It's like a dam that breaks and continues to flood your soul until it's completely washed away. I had no footing. I had no defense. There was no bright side.

With Leisha being here one minute, then gone the very next, I felt desperate to talk to her. I began writing notes and letters to her. As weeks drudged by, the letters evolved into journaling. I needed an outlet where only I could go to express emotion, anger and pain with no worries of anyone hearing, consoling or judging me. But as day after day passed, I lost more and more of myself. I could barely function and every day was a struggle. Hanging by a thread and about to give up on life and myself, Jesus appeared. This is where my journey begins. This vision brought hope and with it questions and a desire for understanding. I knocked… and the door flew open. Behind every flicker of hope though, Satan was there trying to stamp it out by throwing not so nice visions and visitors my way. Through many months of emotional and legal struggles I teetered back and forth between letting the pain and anger overtake me and wanting to find faith and healing.

My journals became a valuable resource when I decided to tell my story. I've placed my pain on display for all to read. Without it, there's no perspective. The faint of heart may struggle with the transparency in which I write but it's that same transparency that allows God to shine through to you. You can expect to be humbled and enlightened by experiencing His Grace as he brings light and purpose to both mine and my daughter's lives.

1 Thessalonians 4:13 NIV

"Brothers and sisters, we do not want you to be uninformed about those who sleep in death, so that you do not grieve like the rest of mankind, who have no hope."

Chapter

One

The Foundation Gives Way

We're all architects of our own lives, personalizing to suit our desires.
Wise is the builder that looks beyond earthly measures.

One afternoon in early July 2010, I wasn't feeling well so decided to lay down on the couch to rest. I'd dozed off a couple of times but awoke hearing my husband working on something in the garage. While lying there, a vision of my daughter, Leisha, suddenly popped into my view. It was black all around her. Her eyes were closed and she had no expression. I jumped up with fear and concern flooding through me. I immediately called her. She didn't answer so I left her a message and sent a text. With no response over the next hour or so, I continued trying to reach her. When she finally called me, I told her what I had seen. She assured me that she was fine. I said, "Leish, I don't want to scare you but it was like someone had really hurt you. It felt serious!" I gave her all the usual reminders, "don't drink and drive, be careful, and don't walk alone." She reassured me that she was fine and said she'd be careful. I asked her to text me when she got home. In the past, when I'd have visions or dreams, they usually came to be within a day or so. I worried about Leisha a lot. She was young, beautiful, outgoing and trusted everyone. After three weeks passed with no incidents, I figured my vision must have just manifested itself because of the stress and worry over my younger daughter, Ashley's, recent health issues.

August 13, 2010: My brother-in-law of thirty years took his own life. Pete was like a true brother to all of us. We were devastated and shocked. On the way to my Mom's house, where everyone was gathering, I called Leisha to tell her Uncle Pete was gone. As with the rest of us, shock, disbelief and sadness immediately hit her. Ashley was still at work so I asked Leish to meet her at her apartment to let her know what happened. I had planned to take Leisha to breakfast the next morning but cancelled in light of this tragedy. It was a decision I would later regret. Ashley was also shocked and upset to hear about Uncle Pete's death. They jumped into the car and headed out to meet up with the rest of the family. Ashley was driving erratically trying to get there quickly. Leisha told her to slow down and stop driving like a crazy person! Even in a crisis, it was just like Leisha to keep a cool head and remain objective. We all met at my Mom's. My poor sister, Donna, was in a state of shock. She and Pete had been together since she was a teenager. We all cried and comforted one another as best we could.

The next day we drove back to my Mom's. Emotions were running high and my niece lashed out in anger from losing her Dad. Ashley and Leisha tried to console their cousin throughout the day but were unsuccessful. As emotions continued to escalate, it was decided that everyone should go home. Leish and a few others remained though to help comfort my sister. Ashley headed home to spend time with her daughter, who had been with her other grandparents. Leish wanted to hang out with friends later in the evening to keep her mind off losing Uncle Pete. She called several friends but only one was available...a young man she'd dated years before, who I'll call "John Doe." He'd come back into her life after her re- cent break up with someone she'd been in a long-term relationship with. He drove up to meet her at Grams. After having a bite to eat, I asked her to come spend the night with us so we could go together in the morning to pay respect to Uncle Pete at the funeral home. She decided she'd rather go out and keep busy. Hugs and kisses were exchanged and she said she'd see me early in the morning. A couple hours later, my niece was still very upset and I received a call from Ashley about a conversation she'd just had with her. After our call ended, I called Leish to be sure she was okay. She had heard from her cousin as well and told me, "We're a close family. We just need to stick together and we'll get through this." We talked for several minutes longer before I told her good night, to be careful and I'd see her in the morning.

August 15, 2010: I was awake very early and had just fixed a bowl of cereal when I heard a knock on the front door. It was a police officer. He said he had bad news for me. My first thought was my brother-in-law. I said, "I know. My brother-in-law took his life

Friday afternoon." He shook his head no. Suddenly worried my sister might have done something to herself because of losing Pete, I asked, "My sister?" He shook his head no again. "There's been an accident." Confusion was replaced with horror as I asked, "Leisha?" "Yes. I'm sorry." I began shaking my head trying to understand what was happening. "No. NO!" I screamed for my husband, Dan. He bolted down the stairs as I fled out the back door screaming and calling to her. I remember pacing and walking frantically in circles trying to comprehend what was happening. This couldn't be real! I don't know how long I was outside nor did I see the officer leave. Heading back in the house to get Dan, I found him on the phone. I paced back and forth, waiting for him to get off the phone. I cried out, "I want to go to her NOW!!!" I grabbed my phone and headed back outside to call my youngest brother, Gary. Hearing his voice, I screamed out those few awful words. I don't remember hanging up and found myself back in the house. Dan was still on the phone. I was threatening to leave without him when two of my brothers arrived. I didn't understand at the time but Dan was trying to find out where she was. I could only think of getting to her. I needed to see her, to hold her, to fix her! My brother, Don, told me to get into his truck. I just stared at him. I thought he was trying to bring me to his house to keep me from driving off on my own. He came over to me and calmly said again, "Get in the truck." I stared at him with confusion. He said, "I'll take you to her." "You promise???" I asked. He assured me he would.

I teetered between sobbing and staring, feeling dazed and confused while we were driving. My mind was racing. My heart was aching. What happened? Did she need me? Was she scared? Where was she? Was she alone? Was she cold? What pain did she feel? Oh, my God!!!!! Where is she??!!! Why???!!! I searched the sky for any sign of her as we drove. Don's voice faded in and out as he talked to me then someone on the phone when trying to find out where she was. I don't recall where we were or how long we'd been driving when I suddenly felt Leisha swoop in and wrap herself around me. I cried out, "She's here! I feel her!" I closed my eyes and heard her say, "I'm sorry, Mom." It lasted only a few moments.

We arrived at the funeral home a short while later. I ran to the door only to find it locked. I pounded on the door and rang the bell. No answer. I tried several times before running around the building looking for another entrance. Dan came to me, trying to calm me down before escorting me to my brother's truck. How could the door be locked??!! Someone within the building must have called the police because they arrived asking what the disturbance was. My oldest brother, Rick, arrived at the same time and had come over to hug me while Don was explaining the situation to the police. We were forced to leave and wait until the funeral director could call us. My daughter was just on the other side of that door. How could they keep me from her??!!! What the hell was happening? What if there was a mistake and she was still alive?! What if she needed me to help her??!!! The police forced us to leave.

It was if I blinked and we were at home again. I have no memory of the ride home. A state trooper was waiting to talk to us. He briefed us on how "John Doe" was apparently intoxicated and speeding, which caused the accident. The car flipped several times, throwing Leisha from the vehicle. He was currently in jail, being held on manslaughter charges. While the trooper was talking, my sister-in-law handed me my cell phone and said it was Ashley. Oh no....Ashley. Does she know?? My head was swirling with shock and confusion. I asked that she talk with her while I finished speaking with the state trooper. I also wanted to compose myself a bit before telling Ash that her sister was gone.

My mind began shutting everyone out. Intervals of reality randomly caught my attention. Pacing in the yard, I'd catch a glimpse of a tree, the flowers or a bird. I stared blankly at them. I remember feeling annoyed at their existence. What had always been a sanctuary filled with beauty and peace, had suddenly become ugly and vulgar to look at. I found myself hating nature and all that it contained. I looked up at the sky, searching for God. My voice was hoarse from crying as I screamed, "F$@& You!" I'd been a fool. Life was a joke! We existed by chance, nothing more. We're as incidental as weeds, dirt or water. It all meant nothing!! My daughter was gone! My beautiful Leisha was gone!! The optimistic view of life I had shown my girls was suddenly worthless. I taught them to be strong, honest, kind and loving. I taught them to stay true to themselves when confronted with challenges and they'd always find their way through. It was all bullshit!! Life was bullshit!!!!! We just occurred by accident, no wonder or magic was behind it. Being good, honest and loving meant nothing!!

I paced and paced and paced. I cried. I stared. I don't remember by whom, but at some point, I was informed that the coroner had to see Leisha before I could and he was unable to do this until the end of the day. How could anyone be that insensitive? How can he make me wait all day? She's "my" daughter! I have a right to be with her! What if she's not really gone?! What if she needs me??!! She's all alone!!!!!! Trying to calm me, I was told that in addition to their examination, they wanted time to clean her up before we saw her. All of this meant I couldn't go to her until 6:00 PM. I couldn't be in the house. I couldn't think. It was torture wondering if she was still alive and in pain. I needed air. I couldn't breathe. Ashley arrived and I ran to her, holding her, sobbing. Panic, shock and pain filled her eyes. The rest of my family arrived over the course of the day. Nieces and nephews drove hours to be with us. Even my poor sister and her children came over. The day was fragmented and time seemed unable to click forward. I felt restrained in a hellish time warp that brought images of my daughter in pain and alone, over and over.

We were waiting at the door of the funeral home when 6:00pm finally arrived. We'd been asked to bring clothing for Leish because they had to remove hers for the examination. I brought my favorite purple micro fleece top that she'd worn in the past. Ashley brought her a pair of her sweat pants. We waited a few more minutes than were allowed in. I ran to her. My beautiful Leisha.... Her face was so swollen it didn't even look like my daughter. She had cuts and bruises. I wanted to hold her but was afraid to hurt her more. I didn't know what was broken. She was cold. Was it really Leisha???!!! Ashley was crying so hard. What do I do?? What do I do??!!! She was cold...Oh my God!!!!!!! How could this be happening? I kissed her forehead and held her face. I wanted to hold her in my arms. What do I do??!! I don't know how long I was there with her. Not long enough. I wish I had stayed. Shock was ruling my mind and body. I leaned in to touch her face with mine and hug her as best I could before turning to leave. I couldn't think. I felt alone. My family was all there but I felt completely alone.

Chapter

Two

Life As We Knew It

Comfort lies in what we know. Our history and routines act as safe boundaries in which we rest our minds and souls.

Growing up in southern Maine, I was one of six children. My Dad refurbished the 1800's home we lived in over the years while managing a small farm and working a full-time job. As if raising us six kids wasn't a big enough load to manage, my Mom worked a fulltime job also. The woman had an endless supply of energy. She was always busy cooking, canning vegetables and relishes each fall, keeping a spotless house and still found time to be involved in our school activities. We all had chores to do but she and my Dad did most of the work. They bought the family snowmobiles, we went camping and enjoyed many family trips. When I was five they purchased a camp on a lake, which brought another level of family activities and gatherings. I barely remember a weekend where our home or camp wasn't filled with grandparents, aunts, uncles, cousins and friends. It was wonderful.

My childhood was quite normal and run of the mill, but I did have a gift that began showing itself when I was only three years old. According to my parents, I was riding in the car with them on the way to funeral services for a friend of theirs that had just passed away. As we pulled into the parking area of the funeral home, I described a statue that was inside the building. They told me years later that I had never been there before and they both wondered how I knew about the statue. This was the beginning of many dreams and visions that would happen prior to them actually occurring. When I was fifteen, I was sitting in my bedroom and had a vision of my parents. They were standing in our kitchen holding each other and crying. An overwhelming sadness hit me and I also began to cry. My mother happened to be putting clean laundry away and saw that I was upset when she came into my room. She asked what was wrong. Somehow I knew from what I'd seen that it meant I was about to lose a brother. After telling her why I was upset, she told me I was wrong and that they were all ok. The next day though, my twenty-one-year-old brother, Greg, was killed in a motorcycle accident. The day after the funeral, I walked into our kitchen to find my parents wearing the same clothing as I had seen in my vision, holding each other and crying.

A few years later, I dreamed another brother's house caught on fire. I described the dream to my Mom the next morning. I explained how my sister answered a phone call in the middle of the night and was screaming up the stairs to all of us that his house was on fire! We looked out my parent's bedroom window to see the flames glowing in the night just a couple miles away. The following evening, each event in order as I had described came true. Gratefully, both he and my sister-in-law escaped without injury.

Another evening, I'd gone to bed and had fallen asleep. At some point in the night, I felt myself lift up and out of bed but could see my body still laying there. I drifted out the window and soon found myself in a vast, dark place. It was so dark that I saw nothing but felt and heard souls asking me who I was, why I was there and to get out as they circled closer to me. When they got too close I suddenly snapped back into my body. I'd been worrying for years that by knowing things before they happened I might be "bad" in some way. This new experience brought relief. The spirits of those I'd encountered felt cold, angry and spiteful. Their apparent dislike of me, told me that I held opposite energy and qualities.

At the age of 4 or 5, I was out in our back yard hanging doll clothes that I'd just washed on a clothesline I'd made with my jump rope. While doing so, I had a vision of a little girl with long, flowing, curly hair. I somehow knew she'd be my daughter and wanted to name her Alicia. I had visions of what she looked like and with those visions, came a sense of what her nature would be. When I was twenty years old, my maternal grandmother, Lona Alura, passed away not long before I was to have this child. Changing the name a bit to flow more smoothly, Leisha Alura Tarbox was born on April

10

15, 1983. Brightness surrounded her from the moment she arrived and she captivated attention without effort. As she grew, she put full effort into everything she touched. Her favorite saying as toddler was, "Tell me all about it." No matter what project or planned event I'd be telling her about, she'd listen intently and asked many questions. This quality remained with her into adulthood. She cared about people and listened to them with her heart.

Time passed and Ashley Alana was born. Leisha took her role as big sister very seriously. When she came to visit me in the hospital just after Ashley's birth, she immediately took on the responsibility of watching over her, tending to her and showering her little sister with kisses. A strong instant bond emerged that followed them throughout the years. As she and Ashley grew, they became best friends.

Leisha and Ashley

Leish loved being in the spotlight. She was always posing for pictures or showing off one way or another. We have many videos of her as a child dancing and twirling as a ballerina, singing or just being interviewed by Mom and Dad on the day's events. Our yard was always filled with kids from the neighborhood. The girls hosted many a tea party and sleep over. Birthday parties were a big ta-doo with treasure hunts, pony rides, clowns, face painting or some other theme to make it fun. It was important to me for the girls to have wonderful memories of their childhood and birthday celebrations were a great way to make them feel special.

The girls were blessed with the opportunity to share their childhood with step brothers, Nick and Dusty. When first meeting, Dusty was 6, Ashley 8, Nick 9 and Leisha was 11 years old. Growing up together, they became very close. Saturday evenings or Sunday afternoons, I'd find them all piled up on the couch watching a movie. Sunday football and the Super Bowl were crazy times at our house. Special fun foods were prepared, foam fingers and collectible helmets set in place and furniture was moved to make room for every- one when jumping to their feet when a good...or more so, a bad play was made.

Nick, Ashley and Dusty, then Dusty, Nick and Leisha

Dusty, Leisha, Ashley and Nick

All four kids were involved with sports. There were soccer games, indoor track, cross country, golf, basketball and baseball games. I loved going to all their events. The girls and I also used to go running and rollerblading together. Eventually part time jobs and dating entered their lives so sporting events faded away. Leisha was the oldest so the first to get her license and a car. The phones were always busy with friends calling, plans being made to hang out and of course what to wear to the many, many proms and dances in high school. Senior prom was a big event for my girls. Several girl friends came to our house to get ready for each of their proms. Hours were spent in the bathroom working on each other's hair and makeup. Upon arrival of their escorts, beauty queens emerged complete with sparkling jewelry, elegant dresses and beaming, beautiful faces. I detained them for as long as I could for a photo session, before they rushed off to have fun and make memories.

Traditions played an important role in our lives. Apple season meant spending an afternoon together picking apples at a nearby orchard, enjoying hot apple crisp with ice cream, apple pies or lots of homemade applesauce. One of my favorite memories was when Leisha picked an apple and part of the stem and a few leaves broke off with it. She bit the stem off and tossed the apple as if it were a grenade and yelled, "Take cover!!" With several dramatic slow motion steps sideways, she dove into a "tuck and roll" pretending it had exploded. We all laughed. Leish had a way of bringing little details to light that most people never notice. Shortly after apple season came the annual pumpkin carving contest with friends and family. As each masterpiece emerged, they were lined up for judging to take place. Once everyone was done, each person voted. Ash- ley often won with some elaborate design or face that she'd carved. Leisha's carvings always got the most laughs because she'd carve one side of the pumpkin with a typical Halloween design and the other with something funny. After candles were placed within each pumpkin to illuminate our designs, lots of pictures were taken with and without the lights on so we could all marvel at how awesome we thought they looked. Something as simple as carving a pumpkin provided so much joy each year.

Bobby and Leisha, then Leish and Ash

Thanksgiving was one of those holidays that we just loved to

14

hang out together. A traditional meal of turkey, homemade stuffing, gravy, rolls, several vegetables, fresh cooked cranberries and several desserts have always been provided in the most festive presentation I could find in the current year's magazines. Our dog Cookie made her way around the table looking for handouts of turkey and stuffing. Being a special member of our family, everyone made sure she had her share of treats. Card games were part of nearly every get together and Thanksgiving was no exception. Our two favorites were "Pit" and "Rat a Tat Cat." I made a conscious effort to take a few moments to soak in their laughter and the chaotic chatter. Nothing made me happier than just being together and everyone having fun.

As much as we loved Thanksgiving dinner, we looked forward to the following weekend when it was time for our annual Christmas tree cutting. Heading to a nearby tree farm, we'd spend an hour or two searching for the best tree on the lot. Leisha gravitated towards the Charlie Brown type trees. Ashley liked to pick out weird shaped ones. Someone else would pick out a stumpy, round one or a giant one with a random branch sticking way out. Leisha usually entertained us by sticking branches in her hair or acting out an improv skit she'd just conjured up. More recent years, videos of our granddaughter running all about were taken while Ya Ya (Aunty Leisha) chased after her. We'd finally find a tree we all agreed on and the sawing began. There's something nostalgic about cutting a Christmas tree. It never gets old. Getting our prize back home, the trunk was trimmed and placed into the tree stand. Holiday music and special snacks made decorating the tree and house fun and festive. Christmas stockings were piled up together waiting to be filled with goodies and our angel figurines were always placed in their traditional spot on the mantle or some elevated shelf so they could keep watch over us.

Leisha with a branch in her hair, then Leish holding Lexy

Over the next few weeks we made cookies and homemade cards with stamps and scrapbooking materials. Christmas day seemed to take forever to arrive. The girls and I spent afternoons together shopping and having lunch out somewhere. Christmas was the one time each year that I'd go all out and spoil everyone. I made a different meal each year, always trying to outdo the last in making it more gourmet and festive. The girls and I liked to perform our dance skit to Madonna's "Santa Baby" that we'd choreographed years before. With presents piled high, decked out with curled ribbons, bows bunched together and lots of holiday colors, emotion always wells up inside as I watch with anticipation when opening that special gift they had wanted so much. That moment, filled with love and happiness, never failed to bring a tear to my eye and a lump in my throat.

Dusty, Ashley, Nick, Leisha, then Nick, Dusty, Ashley, Lexy and Leisha

Springtime brought Easter. Family gathered together for a ham dinner and the annual Easter egg hunt was planned for the kids, which continued well into their teenage years. While most of the eggs contained candy, a few of them held money. Everyone lined up at one door, shouting and laughing hysterically while pushing each other out of the way trying to be first out the door. Once outside, they'd run all around, diving on top of each other to wrestle over an egg that had been found with money in it. They didn't care about the candy or money. They just loved getting a chance to wrestle with each other and act crazy.

Chapter

Three

❦

When It All Began To Change

Even the strongest lose footing when fragmented piece by piece.

In October of 1999, I stopped over to visit my parents one Sunday morning. My Dad grabbed my hand and led me into another room, closing the door. He turned and pulled me close, hugging me so tightly I heard my back crackle. I'd never seen panic in his face before. I asked what was wrong. He said, "You have to help me find your mother." I said, "She's right in the kitchen. I just saw her." He ran out looking for her but walked right pass her. My Dad seldom got sick and had quit smoking years before so that he'd be healthy to enjoy his retirement years. After many hospital visits and consultations with the Alzheimer's association, his diagnosis was inevitable. He was a strong, proud man and was devastated when we told him he had Alzheimer's. He had a rare form of the disease, which accelerated him through all the stages. Though it was heart breaking to see him decline, we were grateful he didn't have to suffer for years as most victims of this disease do. Being placed in a nursing home had always been a concern for both my parents so my Mom kept him home to ensure he received the quality care he deserved. All of us kids pitched in to help. It wasn't long before he became bedridden. To avoid stiff muscles or the chance of getting bed sores, my brothers lifted him in and out of bed and into a wheel chair each day. He was the love of my mother's life. They'd been married for fifty-two years and she still loved him as much as she did when they'd first met. She showered him with affection, attending to his every need. The more weight he lost, the more calories she tried getting into him. Just ten short months after he was diagnosed, we lost him. Nearly forty members of our family were gathered around his bed when he took his last breath. After we were all able to gain some composure, an ambulance was called to transport him to the funeral home. As it led him away, Leisha chased after them, crying out his name. I ran to her and held her, reassuring her that it would be ok.

He was as strong and steady as an oak tree and our Mom was the sunshine that illuminated his presence with warmth and purpose. They were solid, committed and one. Without him, we worried whether she would be able to go forward. We stayed by her side for the first few weeks to help with the transition of the busyness of tending to him night and day to the void and emptiness that now remained. She was truly devastated but impressed us all with her strength and integrity. To this day, many years later, she's still de- voted to our Dad. Her love and commitment to him remains strong.

In 2003 we sold our home in the city and construction began for a cape in the suburbs. Ashley was starting her senior year of high school and Leisha was now twenty years old. With our old home sold and the new one not quite built, we moved in with Gram for a few weeks during the summer. The three of us, two dogs and a cat bunked in the semi-finished basement together sharing a bed and a pull-out couch. It was good timing to be living with Gram so she could watch over Leisha. A grapefruit sized tumor had developed on one ovary and needed to be removed. The surgery went well, but she endured seizures while coming out of the anesthesia. She later told me that she had asked for me but they didn't let me know. It bothered me so much to know she needed me and I wasn't there.

Though it was wonderful to have a place to stay and to save some money while the new house was being built, we were very excited when it was finished and it was time to move in. With no furniture in the house yet, sleeping bags, pasta, Prego sauce and a portable CD player would suffice. We were off to celebrate! We played a Van Morrison CD that evening and when "Into the Mystic" came on, the three of us danced with joy, twirling and swirling about the living room. It became our song. A tribute to our unity and freedom from Gram's basement! We were a team, bonding at a new level that evening. My girls were becoming adults and my role as Mom be- came more balanced between friendship and parenting.

A few months after moving into our new home, we lost our little ten-year-old dog, Brenda. Brenda was Ashley's pet. We all felt the loss but it was hardest on her. She missed sleeping with her as she had every night over the past ten years. Our other dog, Cookie didn't eat for nearly two weeks. She wandered the house whining and looking for her little friend.

Brenda and Cookie

Leisha had been dating Bobby for some time and Ashley was now going steady with a boy as well. The kids enjoyed each other as friends. Having them all under one roof allowed me to watch over them while respecting their growing independence. Bobby is a very talented musician. It was wonderful listening to him play his acoustic guitar, picking away while dinner was cooking or we were all puttering around the house. About a year later, Leisha and Bobby wanted to get a place of their own. I was one of those parents that never wanted my kids to move out. I enjoyed their company and loved sharing their days. We used to leave notes for each other, saying good night, reminding one to wake the other at a certain time, telling them or myself what time we'd be home, etc., always signing with a drawing of a heart and our name. Bobby joined our ritual, later telling me how much he missed those endearing notes after they'd moved out. Leish and I cried when the last few items had been loaded in their car and it was time to go. I was going to miss her. Thankful that Ashley and her boyfriend were still at home, the empty nest syndrome was delayed for a while longer.

About a year after she'd moved out, my job at a large insurance corporation was eliminated along with thirty-two others in my department. The company had been consolidating in an attempt to cut costs for some time. I burned through most of my retirement savings the first two years trying to keep up with the mortgage, taxes and bills before deciding to sell the house in the summer of 2006. Of course, that happened to be when the housing market began to decline so my profit ended up being smaller than it could have been. The girls had broken up with their boyfriends so decided to get an apartment together in Portland. It was a charming old building and in a great location which meant they'd be close to their friends, college, their jobs and shopping. They loved it. Leisha had met some new friends from Romania and other foreign countries. With feelings developing for one of the boys, she invited him and two others up to Gram's to go swimming and tubing on the lake. The following is a short story she wrote for a college class about this day at the lake. I've changed the names of her friends to protect their privacy.

September 5, 2006

I open my eyes after a peaceful night's sleep. I squint as I try to focus on my bedroom window. As I untangle myself from the sheets I feel a cool August breeze hit my shoulders. Just as the weathermen predicted, it was a cloudy morning, but my hopes of a warm, sunny, Saturday still held strong, because I had planned a trip to Little Ossipee Lake.

After rummaging through my assortment of bathing suits, I get dressed and head downstairs. Just then my phone rings; it's Ionel. He's calling to finalize plans. Having already talked to Iancu and Cosmin, they are just as optimistic about the weather as I am. Before hanging up the phone he requests breakfast and as always, I say yes. Anything for my three favorite men. Impatient for them to arrive, I stand over the stove watching the sausage and eggs sizzling in the pan. The smell of it all makes my mouth start to water. Just as I shut the burner off, I hear the front door slam. Cosmin is the first to arrive and I truly think he's more anxious than I am. We sit to eat our steaming breakfast and shortly after are accompanied by Ionel and Iancu.

A quick clean up and we are out the door. I crawl into the back seat with Cosmin, leaving us with limited extra space. He puts his arm around me, like usual, and I rest my head on his shoulder. As the thumping music plays I can hear him singing in my ear. Music is his passion. And I giggle to myself, because I'm exactly where I want to be.

As we depart from the city, following long winding country roads, I notice the dominate color of green surrounding us. For a moment, I drown out the sound of techno music. Closing my eyes, I wonder if they, too, feel that this world is an amazing place.

We turn down the final dirt road finding my sister's boyfriend greeting us on the four-wheeler. As we pull up to my grandmother's house and get out of the car, I feel the combination of relief and nervousness, hoping my friends will enjoy their stay. Just then, Gram comes out to see us, cheerful as always. Going down the line shaking hands as I introduce her to my gorgeous European friends. She has a little trouble pronouncing their names, and we all get a little chuckle out of it. We follow her to the bottom of the hill where we set out chairs in front of the water. It's about 11:00 AM now, and everything seems a little too quiet for this hour. In the distance I see only one boat; they are fishing and evidently are having no luck. I comment multiple times about how rare it is for the lake to be so vacant. This place didn't feel the same. To entertain ourselves, we decide to all take turns riding the four-wheeler. I climb on the machine, feeling the power at my fingertips as I tear down the road and out of sight. Eventually, I force myself to return to the house, knowing I could have driven carefree for hours. Instead, I lead the four of us to the end of the dock where we prepare ourselves for the cool water rush. I dive, surprised to find that the sensation on my skin was refreshing and warm. We swim to the middle of the cove where I float on my back looking at the sky. The sun is still fighting the clouds.

Back on land, we cluster back at the group of chairs, conversing about what's important in life. As the others eventually change the subject, Cosmin continues to elaborate on religion. He expresses his devotion to God, and how he feels privileged to be living the life that has been chosen for him. His words encourage me to have even more faith in the Heavenly Father.

He and I take off to the basement and play a few rounds of pool. He loves playing and is great at it, yet he lets me win all three games. I think to myself as he's entertaining me with his great sense of humor. What an amazing person. His words show intelligence; his talents are unlimited. I felt honored to share a room with such a kind, respectful, energetic man. His handsome face reveals such innocence. He circles the pool table drawing near to me. Stepping behind me he puts his arms around me once again. I can feel his warm bare stomach against my skin. His towering structure seems to enclose mine, and it's comforting.

My phone rings and I race to meet the call. It's my mother, and she's 10 minutes away. Upon arrival, she agrees to drive the boat, so I scurry to get the tube inflated. Needing help, I call to Ionel and Iancu, who were both sitting at the edge of the dock watching Cosmin swim. Assuming it doesn't take three people to inflate the tube, I exit the garage, confused to find my mom speeding off in the boat. Something was wrong. Where's Cosmin? I darted to the end of the dock. Waiting for my mother's return, we all stand in denial. Those seconds seemed like an eternity.

Screaming frantically, call 911! He's been hit by a boat! She jumps out of the boat, and Ionel takes her place. The boat is back out in the middle of the lake before I get a chance to board. I start to tremble as I turn to Iancu. My determination to be at Cosmin's side influences me to steal the neighbors jet ski. No keys! Now what?!

Miraculously, I spot a woman on her jet ski, and I repeatedly shout until she recognizes my call. I throw myself on the back, and we flew to the other side of the lake. It felt like miles. My stomach in knots, I jump to shore, finding Cosmin's motionless body surrounded by an audience of locals. I drop to my knees, running my hands over his colorless face. I talk to him, encouraging him to stay with us. I pick out a voice in the blur of it all: "He's still got a pulse."

25

I continue talking with Cosmin, but his eyes rolling to the back of his head tells me he's not listening. As I sit in shock, I ask God to spare his life, the life of one who worships His work. How can He choose someone who has so much to offer? Still communicating to Cosmin, Ionel and I hold his cold hands, which once had strength to hold me, too.

Moments later the paramedics finally arrive. We all stand by with overwhelming anticipation. They pause to inform us that nothing can be done. He's not breathing on his own, and doesn't have a heartbeat. In addition, he's lost all his blood from the large wound that stretches down his midsection, which explains the yellowish gray tint of his skin.

Hatred takes over my voice as I beg for them to fix the problem. Bring my friend back into this world. I can't let go; it's not real. As they carry him to the stretcher, I shut his eyes for him, and run my hands through his damp hair. Cosmin lays there lifeless next to the ambulance, and while nothing else seems to matter to me at this point, the audience has returned to their normal lives, something that this beautiful creature, who was lying before me, will never do again.

The car ride home felt awkward. In the seat where Cosmin once traveled, now sits only his belongings. Mystery has filled my head with questions that will never be answered. What if I had played one more game of pool with Cosmin? What if I had hugged him one minute longer? He would have been one minute away from that propeller, and safe in the car with the rest of us.

Not a day goes by that the scene doesn't replay itself in my head. And only in my dreams do I get to see his face and hear his voice.

Leisha was devastated, feeling guilty and to blame for his death by inviting him to the lake that day. We all felt there should have been something different we could have done to prevent this horrible accident, rehashing the "what ifs' over and over and over. She struggled for a very long time before accepting that it wasn't her fault. It was his time. Her perspective on life changed, though. She began seeing life with more depth and direction. She'd also told me that she'd begun seeing eyes at night when she closed her own. They were just watching her. Both the girls and I had past experiences seeing those that had passed on so I felt that she was just experiencing this on a different level since losing her friend. We both shrugged it off at the time. I would later begin experiencing the same thing wishing I had talked to her more about it.

Excerpt from Leisha's diary:
" Don't fight the silence and don't fight the everlasting urge to fight life. Life is a challenge. It's all about fighting. Reach for what's right, right in your mind because that's what's best for you. Don't give up. Fight till your dying day. Prove your reason."

Just as we were starting to feel relief from the devastation of losing Cosmin, I decided to take a tumble on a hill in the back yard one late afternoon. With a rock rolling underfoot, I fell backwards and hit my head. Being the tough gal that I think I am, I figured I was fine. Two days later, upon standing up, the pain would surge in my head with my neck and spine curling backwards on its own, pulling me with it. My knees would buckle and I was unable to stand. My vision was now distorted, seeing double of everything. An x-ray revealed a fractured skull and an MRI confirmed a concussion. By waiting so long to go to the hospital, the swelling had begun to travel down into my neck and spine. When I fell, my head hit so hard that it threw my brain forward, cutting the frontal lobes in several places from banging against the ridge of the brow bone in my skull. My husband later told me that I had passed out when I had fallen and he had been trying to bring me to for a couple of minutes before I regained consciousness. I have no memory of it. The pain was so bad by this point I could no longer think nor function. With a smorgasbord of IV drugs prescribed, I was admitted. Two days later I awoke having no recollection of what day it was or how I came to wear a hospital Johnny. I was released later that afternoon with prescriptions of pain killers and steroids. It took about four weeks for the double vision and temporary memory issues to subside. After three months, the dizzy spells stopped and I was finally back to normal.

In 2007, Ashley found out she was going to have a baby. She was sick through most of her pregnancy needing medication to keep food down but otherwise felt good. At the end of her 8th month, though, she developed Preeclampsia so the doctors induced labor when her blood pressure shot up to a dangerous level. The hypertension caused her arms and legs to jerk uncontrollably. She was given medication to reduce the blood pressure but the doctor warned us that it may cause hemorrhaging during delivery. My husband didn't get to have children of his own so Ashley welcomed him into the delivery room to witness his granddaughter's birth. He felt uncomfortable with invading her privacy so he declined at first.

After a bit of coaxing, we finally talked him into it. At first he kept his focus on a corner of the room but quickly became enthralled when the baby's head began to crown. All he saw from that point on was the miracle of life unfolding in front of him. Leisha, myself and the baby's father were by her side as well. We each took an arm and a leg, supporting Ash during contractions and pushing. None of the complications mattered when it was time for her baby to enter the world. She couldn't wait and cried out with the last two pushes, "I want my baby!!" The extra nurses brought in to the room took immediate action when the hemorrhaging did in fact begin. It all happened so quickly that I didn't have time to let what I saw resonate, thank goodness. Tears of joy streamed down her cheeks when little Alexis Abigail was placed in her arms. Leisha and I both leaned in from each side. Love, pride and joy radiated from each of us. Ashley couldn't take her eyes of her little girl...a beautiful young mother holding her baby. Other parents and family members were welcomed in. More tears were shed for the new beautiful child in

our lives, for the love reflecting in Ashley's tired face and with relief that she was ok. Now that it was over, Leisha became overwhelmed with emotion. Seeing her sister struggle with all the complications and the emotion of childbirth itself caused her to feel light headed. She had to sit down. After a few moments though, she was back up and gazing at little Lexy. She looked up at Ash with love and pride and uttered, "Aunty."

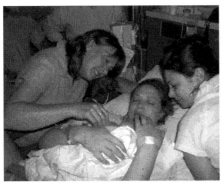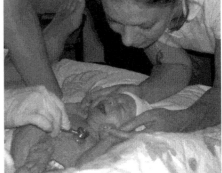

Wanda, Ashley holding Lexy & Leisha, then Leisha looking at Lexy

Excerpt from Leisha's diary:

2009: "Pete Kilpatrick Band plays on my radio in a line of traffic sitting in frustration hurrying to class and stuck behind a draw bridge. A man steps out of his car and grabs his boy from the seat behind. They point into the distance as he shows his son the tug boat that slowly creeps by. Pete sings "With love in our eyes, we open our heart, the colors all seem so bright..." and as the man and son take their places behind the wheel and the draw bridge goes down, suddenly I'm not in such a rush anymore."

A few months after Lexy was born, Ashley began not feeling well and her bladder was bothering her. A few tests and doctor visits later, she was diagnosed with over active bladder. During testing she mentioned a buzzing she had begun feeling in her neck and that her left arm and leg would go numb occasionally. The combination of bladder issues and these new symptoms, the doctor ordered an MRI concerned she might have MS. MS was ruled out but a brain tumor was revealed. Many tests and consultations later with the doctors and surgeons, it was determined that she had a cell spreading type of tumor versus a mass. A craniotomy was scheduled for the end of March, 2010. Two weeks before her surgery, my little dog, Cookie, (and dear friend of ten years) had an unexpected seizure. We lost her just 4 days later. I was devastated but had no time to grieve her loss. I had to stay focused on Ashley.

Surgery day was stressful on so many levels. There was a fear of losing Ashley in surgery or to cancer. There was a fear of her coming out of surgery paralyzed, not knowing any of us or having any quality of life. There was the fear of the surgery itself, not only for Ashley who had to undergo this awful procedure but to see my child go through such an invasive and violating experience. We try to protect our children all through their lives from sickness and injury. How does this happen? She was only twenty-four years old and should be healthy! I wondered if I could have done something differently while she was growing up. Was it the foods she ate, exposure to something? So many thoughts went through my mind but I couldn't find an answer.

Watching them wheel her down the hallway and into the operating room seemed to occur in slow motion. My heart was pounding and I felt sick. It was out of my hands. I felt frustrated and anxious. I wanted to take away her worry and pain. It was difficult to just sit and wait. I watched the monitors constantly hoping to see a change in her status. I got up and checked with the waiting room attendant several times but no news. Medical staff came and went with no update. My stomach was in knots. The waiting room was filled with family members who tried to keep me preoccupied with conversation. They talked but I barely heard their words. Ash had been so worried she wasn't going to be there for her daughter as she grew. She was afraid she wouldn't make it through the surgery or that something would go wrong and she'd wind up a vegetable or not recognize any of us. She had pictures professionally taken of her and Lexy together just a few days prior to surgery. During the photo shoot, Ash kissed her on the head and cheek over and over. She wanted Lexy to know how much Mommy loved her little girl, in case she wouldn't be able to tell her later on.

Four agonizing hours later, the surgery was finally over. The surgeon stopped in the recovery room to see how she was doing while coming out of the anesthesia. Ashley extended her hand to shake his and said, "You're a good man!" We chuckled because she was still groggy and out of sorts but I knew what she was trying to say. She recognized us and could speak and move. That's all that mattered to her at that moment. A section of her skull had been removed to gain access to the affected area of her brain. More than half of her front, right lobe had been removed. The surgeon took a larger portion than he thought had been affected, reaching into healthy tissue, hoping to get all the bad cells. The bone was put back into place with titanium screws and her scalp stitched back into place. Ashley had envisioned a large turban of gauze on her head after surgery and was horrified to think this would be her look until hair could grow back. The surgeon was able to avoid shaving her hair off. She was so grateful to see it still in place! The weight of surgery now off one shoulder, the other was lifted when the biopsy later revealed there was no cancer. It also confirmed the type of tumor as an astrocytoma, low grade glioma. This type of tumor has a high probability of growing back so MRI's would be needed every three months for the first couple of years, then every six months for a few more years then annually for a few more. These were needed to watch for any signs of growth so immediate action could be taken if found. If it did grow back and was left untreated, it could turn cancerous as well as affect normal functioning.

When released from the hospital only two days later, I moved in with Ash for two weeks to take care of her and Lexy. Whenever Leisha wasn't at work or school, she was there by her side as well. Ashley loved the attention, soaking it in for as long as she could. She had to use a portable commode for a while after surgery be- cause of the headaches, dizziness and seizures. She still loves telling the story of asking Leisha to empty the potty for her one afternoon. When Leish came into the bedroom to find only three "pebbles" in the potty, she said, "Really, Ash?!" They both laughed, which made Ashley's head hurt more! On the way to the hospital the morning of surgery, Leisha had heard a song on the radio that reminded her of Ashley. She told her that the words of "lipstick stains on the front lobe of my left side brains" and "my soul sister, I don't wanna miss a single thing you do tonight" caught her attention. They truly are "Soul Sisters." She and Ash have always been close but this ordeal brought them even closer together

Ashley's seizures slowly faded and her health steadily improved. She'd told us that if she made it through surgery, she wanted her, Lexy, Leisha and I to all go to the Boston aquarium for Mother's Day so that's just what we did the following spring. It was a rainy day but it didn't matter. We laughed and joked on the ride down, chatting non-stop. Leish dragged her current beau along. He was a good sport putting up with all of us women. We got lost a couple of times trying to find our way around Boston, laughing when we realizedwe'd circled around the same area twice. We could see the aquarium but was having a hard time finding the right exit! After finally arriving, we took our time looking at all the exhibits. It was a wonderful day.

Before her surgery, Ash had confided to me she didn't think she'd make it to see another birthday. When her next birthday did arrive, Leisha and I planned a special day to celebrate the continuation of her life and how bravely she'd faced such an intimidating situation. Leisha picked her up and they drove to our house together. The timing was perfect, arriving just after all the guests had. Seeing confusion on her face, we told her the party was for her. It took a few seconds longer to resonate before becoming over-whelmed with emotion. She was totally surprised. Tears filled her eyes when we all sang happy birthday to her.

By September, the doctors told her that she could go back to work part time as long as she took it slow and didn't exert herself or lift anything heavy. She had become certified as a Phlebotomist and had applied for a job at a local lab not long before she found out about her tumor. The day before her surgery, she was offered the phlebotomy position at a local medical office. Trying to reassure her, we told her it was a positive sign that the surgery would go well. Just a few short months later, she'd also be struggling with the loss of her sister. Her Dad and I encouraged her to go to work, in hopes it would help her heal and find direction again. Her new employer worked with her to ease her into the job, allowing her short days at first until she could gain her strength back.

Chapter

Four

Spiraling Downward

*What binds us to life when deprived of the elements
that fuel our minds and souls?*

The funeral was scheduled. I spent hours compiling pictures of Leish onto a CD to be used as a slideshow during services at the funeral home. I gathered framed pictures of her to place throughout the rooms as well. I wanted her to be everywhere. During the next meeting with the funeral director, he asked if we were going to go with cremation or embalming. How does a parent choose such a thing? Embalming is such a barbaric process but to choose to have your child's body burned?! It was the most painful, agonizing decision I have ever made. The girls and I had a conversation about this at on time and Leish had said she preferred cremation, so after her Dad, Ashley and I talked about it for a few minutes, together that's what we decided on. As if those choices weren't torturous enough, we were then asked to choose a box to transport her in, then to choose an urn for her ashes. He then asked us for a picture and verse to be placed on a memory card. Each question he asked I looked at him in confusion. My mind and ears weren't functioning properly. His words seemed muffled and my mind was foggy. It was as if it were all playing out in slow motion. Each moment was an effort just to exist. Each decision and step forward seemed forced and non-directional.

I no longer slept. To avoid keeping my husband awake all night too, I began utilizing the spare bedroom. Every night I'd just lay there thinking, then crying, then thinking some more. The night before the services, I heard Leisha's voice. She was crying and said, "She going without me!" I sat up in bed. My heart told me she was referring to Ashley being able to live life without her. "I know. I'm so sorry, honey!" I desperately looked about my room for her listening intently, but saw nor heard anything more. My poor Leisha...where is she? How do I help her???!!!

Many years ago, when my brother Greg passed away, my father purchased several burial plots in a cemetery near our home town. He didn't buy any for my sister and I, thinking that someday we'd want to be laid to rest with our husband's families. My father, brother and both maternal grandparents rest there now. Their spot is in a section that overlooks the river, with beautiful trees, shrubs and flowers surrounding them with serenity. My brother Don

36

offered his plot for Leisha. My love, respect and gratitude will forever be with him for this gift. It brought such comfort and peace to know she would rest next to my Dad.

Visiting services were held on Wednesday evening. My husband had obtained some sedatives from my doctor and talked me into taking one prior to leaving our home. I don't know that I would have been able to function at all that evening without it. Though I felt numb and empty, I went through the motions, greeting everyone as they filtered in. Every room was crowded with family, friends and co-workers. People I hadn't seen in years came by to show their sup- port. My whole family was there. My sister and her kids were also, even after enduring the loss of their husband and father just days before. Nieces and nephews brought tissues and water, constantly checking to see if they could do anything for me. We were later told by the funeral director that he'd never seen that many people attend a service before. He said cars lined the streets for many blocks. A line of friends and family that lasted for hours went out the door and quite a distance down the sidewalk. Leisha touched so many lives. She made all of us better people just by knowing her.

The next day, we gathered in a stone chapel within the cemetery. One of Leisha's oldest and dearest friends sang Beyoncé's "Halo." Leisha loved this song and it now brought a new meaning than it had before. It was sung beautifully with deep love and emotion. It was a touching tribute. Leish's recent boyfriend then got up to speak. Adding some lighthearted humor here and there he shared stories of their time together. The chapel wasn't big enough to support all the friends and family that had come to pay tribute.

Many gathered outside, listening as best they could. After the services were completed, we moved to her final resting place. Reverend Howe spoke a few kind words, said a prayer, and then blessed our Leisha. Ashley brought a music box they'd had since childhood. It was topped with a porcelain figurine of an angel covering a sleeping child with a blanket. As she, Nick and Dusty moved closer to say goodbye to their sister, Ash laid the music box down so it could be buried with her. Their sorrow and burden overflowed into me. I rushed over, wrapping my arms around all three of them. We stood huddled together in shock, lost and broken.

My maternal grandmother and grandfather had passed away just before Leisha was born. They appeared to me in a vision shortly after their passing. They were in a warm, sunny field holding hands and smiling at me. As far back as I can remember, I don't recall seeing either of them without their eye glasses, however, neither were wearing them in my vision. That was the last time I'd seen them until having a vision of my grandmother just three weeks before Leisha's accident. I had also recently begun feeling my brother Greg nearby. One evening I awoke to see a ball of white twinkles gathered together next to my bed, just in front of the nightstand. I dismissed it the next day thinking I had been dreaming but looking back, I now know the twinkles was that of an angel coming to me in anticipation of what was to occur. Loved ones had also begun appearing, knowing I would soon need them. Just three weeks later, Leish would be lying on the dark highway at 1:50am struggling to stay with us, but losing the fight. Why didn't the vision I was given have more detail so that I could have prevented this from happening?!! What was the purpose if I couldn't do anything about it??!

Leisha had driven to Gram's before going out that evening and had parked her car in my brother's driveway, who lives next to my Mom. She'd ridden with "John Doe" when they went out that evening so her car was still there. I wanted it home with me. This car was her pride and joy. She was so proud when she'd bought it. Driving it to my house was emotional. She last sat where I was now sitting. She was the last person to touch the steering wheel. Touching it now myself was like touching her hands. Back at my house, I found her CD's and a few other personal items. Her Dad had helped her buy the car. Knowing how much she loved it, he couldn't bear to sell it to anyone. He later paid off the loan and now keeps her car at his home.

Emails from Leisha's friends had been pouring in expressing condolences, sending pictures and sharing how much Leisha meant to them. Every picture was priceless. I looked at each of them over and over. Her Facebook page was also being tagged with many pictures and shared experiences or kind thoughts of her. I checked it often, saving copies of any new photos I could find. I read through her emails, soaking in as many precious moments of her life as I could. Ashley was also receiving a lot of comments and pictures on her Facebook page. She'd begun posting notes to Leisha every night. Her words portrayed her pain. She was trying to connect with her sister and hold on to what they'd had.

August 27, 2010: A friend of Leisha's forwarded me an email from John Doe. It had made its way through a couple of people before she'd received it, asking that they get it to me. It was full of denial and excuses. No apologies, no remorse. I passed it on to our attorney.

Leisha's landlord had been a patient at the rehab facility where she worked a couple of years back and had become friends with him. He experienced a set-back a year or so later and was back at the rehab center so they became reacquainted. He lived upstairs in a duplex that he owned and told her that his downstairs tenant was moving out after sixteen years. The apartment needed a lot of work. Offering it to Leisha at a very reasonable monthly rate, he asked if she'd be willing to clean it up if he supplied the materials. Before deciding, she and I went over to assess the condition. We stood in shock. It had a nice layout and the structure revealed character but it appeared as though it hadn't been cleaned in years. The walls were dark, dingy and the whole apartment smelled of cigarettes, grease and other unpleasant odors. Leisha embraced the challenge. Over the next several weeks, broken windows were replaced, carpet was torn out and every inch of the apartment was scoured. She then applied a coat of sealer before repainting all walls and ceilings. She filled dumpster after dumpster with broken, rusty appliances, old dilapidated furniture and trash that had piled up in the basement and garage. She cleaned and trimmed up the yard, fixed the stone walkway and built a fire pit and a wooden bench to sit on. The transformation was amazing. Windows that you could barely see through before were now clear. Sunlight brightened and warmed each room. Her color choices, furniture and décor added to the charm of this newly revived living space. I was so proud of her. She was proud of herself.

Ashley and I drove to her apartment a couple days after the accident. I looked around trying to soak in her presence. I walked from room to room, desperately wanting her to be there as I turned a corner. A few dishes sat in the sink. Her clothes she'd worn just days before lay on the bathroom floor. I walked into the bedroom, laid down on her bed and rested my head on her pillow. The pillow "her head" had rested on just two nights before. I wanted to feel her....to hold her, to smell her curly brown hair. Joining me on the bed, Ashley and I lay there for quite some time holding hands and sobbing. I didn't want to leave. I wanted to feel her through the sheets, blankets and pillows that had touched her skin and brought her comfort as she slept. A clear red colored plastic tumbler that still held a bit of water, sat on the nightstand. Where is my daughter?? Did she cease to exist? How could this be?? How could such a beautiful young woman who loved life, who anchored me to life, be gone? A veil that I had subconsciously created through my life had been cruelly ripped away with no warning or consideration. Without it, the perception I had come to know as "life" now revealed the façade I had created from selected idealistic fantasies. Life no longer had purpose. I wanted to escape into sleep and not wake until she came home. But sleep did not come. Nor did Leisha. Only silence and emptiness remained.

August 30, 2010: *I picked up your purse today from the towing company that's holding John Doe's car. Your purse. Your personal belongings. Your keys. Your phone. It's broken now. Some items were shattered, some still intact. I will keep them close and together always. They were yours, Leish.*

September 2010: Packing up your belongings today tore at wounds that are still raw. It was so painful. *Each item that was placed in a box felt like we were saying you had no importance, no longer had value...like a puzzle when it's pulled apart becomes a fragmented story. I want your picture to remain whole. Your furniture, dishes and décor had come together through the years, creating a comfortable beginning for the life you were planning. In your refrigerator was a tofu and black bean dish that you had made. I ate a little at a time over the next couple of days trying to appreciate every bite. Money was tight for you, balancing school, an apartment and a car payment. You paid for those ingredients. You prepared this dish and had eaten of the same. One apple and fresh baby spinach were also in your fridge. Ashley and I later shared them in what we refer to as "Leisha salads." Healthy, organic and gourmet. Every bite was eaten with love and appreciation.*

I was so proud of the woman you'd become. You were so full of life. Ashley and I kept many of your personal things with us. I wear your robe and slippers as I sit here tonight. It helps me feel close to you. Ashley wears your clothes and jewelry with pride. It comforts her as well. We touch them with tenderness, appreciating that you picked them out, that they represent you...your flare, your taste. Your purse and recently worn clothes lay on a chair in my bedroom. I breathe you in now and then while hugging them. The beautiful quilt you made is spread across the bed. Your diaries, drawings and dream house clippings you had collected are amongst other items I can't bear to put away. You created such a presence to so many, bringing sunshine, creativity, positive energy and joy to all that knew you.

Leisha wore two particular rings together on one finger almost every day, only changing them out for costume jewelry now and then when going out with her friends. One is platinum with a blue sapphire stone and four small diamonds, two on each side. The other is platinum also with eleven small diamonds set side by side within the band. She wore them so often that I was surprised to find them sitting in her jewelry box. Ash and I each wear one now. It helps us feel close to her and symbolize our unity. We'll wear them throughout the rest of our lives.

October 22, 2012: It's taken me weeks to write the above few paragraphs. Recalling each event has been difficult. My body trembles at times. Sorrow erupts from deep within as old wounds break open, leaving me sobbing for long periods of time. I had to set the book aside for a few weeks in an attempt to regain some level of footing. While sitting in bed last night, I stared at my laptop trying to gather enough courage to pick it up and begin writing again. After a few deep breaths, I turned it on and began re-reading those few pages last entered. Editing a bit here and there, an hour was all I could manage. Shutting off the lights and closing my eyes, a cross immediately appeared to me with blue twinkles sparkling on each side of the cross's horizontal beam. Several smaller white and salmon twinkle lights were at the bottom and top. There was a large beam of blue light shining in from the top, left side of the cross, extending down towards me. It was wider at the bottom than the top. I then saw an angel with a perfectly shaped halo above her head. Nothing more was shown to me. I dozed off after some time but tossed and turned all night. Lying in bed this morning, a vision of a large body of water appeared. I saw only water, no shore nor sky. It was deep and slightly moving. A moment later, a cross appeared. The background was filled with Leisha's favorite color, light teal. I kept asking for clarification on what this meant but saw nothing more. Being exhausted from lack of sleep, I left for work an hour later than usual. Once in my car, I turned the radio on to a Christian station I now listen to regularly. A discussion was underway about death. The speaker explained how we all have to face it, no matter how young, old, rich or famous. He spoke of how Joshua led the Israelites over the Jordan River to the promise land of Canaan and that water symbolizes death as we cross over into heaven...the true promise land. The Jordan River is where Jesus was baptized. The Holy Spirit descended upon him at that time, with the voice of God from heaven acknowledging Jesus as his son. It's also where the people of Israel had to cross in order to obtain freedom in the promise land. God knows I'm struggling and provided a vision and message for me. He felt my pain and wanted me to understand that Leisha had to face death. He was helping me understand it was her time to take the journey to heaven by crossing her river.

Deuteronomy 11:31: NIV
"You are about to cross the Jordan to enter and take possession of the land the Lord your God is giving you."

Chapter

Five

❧

Through Layers of Debris,
A Flicker of Light

Even the smallest of hope can lead us.

The day after Leisha's accident, a state trooper had told us that the State of Maine was pressing manslaughter charges against "John Doe" and provided us with the district attorney's information. During our first meeting with the DA, we were briefed on the process and the details of "John Doe's behavior that evening began to unfold. Both the DA and the victim's advocate that we met with were extremely kind, helpful and displayed sincere warmth and emotion when speaking of our loss. Being sensitive to our loss, words were carefully chosen while answering our multitude of questions. The DA told us that John Doe had been released from jail when the $40,000 bail had been paid by his parents. His bail conditions stated not to possess or use any alcoholic beverages or illegal drugs and not to operate any motor vehicle under any circumstances. A no contact order would also be drawn up.

With the help from family members and friends, an attorney was secured to represent us for the lawsuit side of the proceedings. During our first meeting, we were asked multiple questions and then were briefed regarding the process. He provided some information on events that had occurred and explained that a private investigator would begin doing research. He also asked if we could try to collect names of witnesses that may have seen Leisha and John Doe out that evening. We provided information needed to draw up personal representative paperwork and were told that we'd be receiving copies of the death certificate in the next few days. The meeting ended and as we walked away, new thoughts were emerging that left me even more unsettled, confused and angry. How did we get here?

Shortly after we'd met our attorney, a friend of Leisha's let me know that she'd found out that a police officer on duty the evening of the accident had observed John Doe's display of anger toward Leisha. He had seen them while they were standing on the sidewalk outside of a pizza parlor. He saw John Doe got into his car and then saw Leisha get in shortly after. He then observed "John Doe" waving his arms around in the car while yelling at her. As he began to approach the vehicle, "John Doe" sped off, turned the corner and was gone. I asked her if he had followed them or done anything about the altercation he had witnessed. She said he had done nothing. A few days later, I met with his lieutenant. I communicated that I felt the officer should have taken action and that had he done so, Leisha may still be here with us. He promised to do some investigating and get back to me. Several days later, I called for an update only to find that he couldn't give me any information because the case was un- der investigation. I contacted our civil attorney and explained the situation but was informed that both the officer and the municipality in which he worked were immune from suit. He said that under Maine law and the Tort Claims Act, which is a public obligation duty doctrine, the officer and city he serves are protected from lawsuit. The premise being, I was told, was that public servants, such as police officers, often have to make decisions while under duress so cannot be held liable if not taking the actions we feel they should have. Leisha and John Doe were in a town well known for night clubbing. The officer should have logically concluded that alcohol would most likely be a factor, especially that late at night. In addition, he observed John Doe's aggressive behavior as well as him speeding off in his car. To me, it was an easy assessment that should have been made and acted upon. Isn't that their job? This information was just one of the many aftershocks to come, burying me deeper under the debris of shattered beliefs.

Another upsetting situation was revealed when two separate CNA's contacted me at separate times. They each provided the same information, saying that there were two doctors that had come upon the accident, as they had, and stopped to help. One of the women said Leisha had begun having difficulty breathing so she tried to help her. She went on to say that when the ambulance arrived, the doctors provided their credentials (one being head of Anesthesiology at one major hospital and the other head of Pulmonary and Critical Care at another major hospital) and asked for an intubation kit but the EMT refused. She said the doctors had begun administering CPR on Leisha but the EMT just stood there arguing that he should now be in control. The other CNA confirmed this information and added that the he walked very slowly, showing no urgency or regard for the patient. I provided this information to our attorney who promised to investigate and secure documentation for us.

Over the next several days, I robotically managed Leisha's affairs. Each item took an enormous amount of energy and emotional strain. I contacted her employer, her landlord and the college she'd been attending. I went to the post office to have her mail sent to me, called the utility company, got copies of her insurance policy and began communications with the provider that held her student loan. Most difficult of all was shutting off her phone service and closing out her bank accounts. I wanted her phone to stay on. Shutting it off felt as though I had accepted she was gone. I'd been calling her number just to hear her voicemail recording and had sent a text message to her phone now and then when I felt desperate to talk with her or see her. Shutting off her phone service meant shutting off one more piece of her life, of my connection to her. I could barely speak when I met with a gentleman at the mall kiosk. Pushing down the emotion that was welling up, it took several attempts to communicate why I was there. I was grateful for the brevity of this difficult task and the kindness he showed me. I retreated to my home and withdrew to my bedroom for the rest of the day. I felt as though I had done something wrong or hurtful to Leisha, like I was shutting off her communication or access to us. The emptiness deepened further.

I forced myself to go to the bank a few days later. Leish had a small credit line at the bank and I didn't want them to think she was ignoring her responsibilities. Both girls still had the same bank accounts I'd opened for them when they were very young. The employees at the credit union had come to know them and greeted them by name whenever they stopped in. The history and personal connection of it all now made my task more difficult. Leish worked three different part time jobs trying to keep up with her bills while in school. She worked hard to keep it all afloat. It felt like I was wiping all her efforts and livelihood away. At times, I just stood there, staring blankly. Every breath was literally forced. When asked a question, my thoughts were incomplete and foggy. Her balance of only a few hundred dollars was withdrawn and placed into the estate account that would later go to her sister. Her account was closed. There are no words to describe the anguish I felt.

Every day was becoming more bleached and faded. Unless relevant to Leisha, I heard nothing. I felt nothing but pain, emptiness and frustration. Not only did I lose the most cherished gift I could ever have...my child...but my foundation had crumbled beneath me with no warning. My little friend Cookie had been abruptly taken from me, there was Ashley's surgery and pending health concerns, my brother-in-law took his own life, Leisha was now gone... I had no footing and no longer cared. I didn't want to be here anymore. Ashley came to mind but grief quickly consumed any rationale and left me empty and with no direction, no hope. Alcohol numbed me just enough to quiet the re-runs of Leisha's accident playing over and over and over in my mind. I kept envisioning her being thrown from the car, needing me...I wasn't there to protect her. It was destroying me.

One evening, I drove down a dirt road that led to a very large parcel of land and parked my car. The sun had gone down and night had already set in. Sitting in silence I drank from a bottle of alcohol I'd brought with me. My mind raced. I cried. I screamed. I drank. I thought of the bottle of sedatives in my purse. I cried and screamed some more then sat in silence. Numb. Empty. A woman's voice broke the silence. I could hear it echoing throughout the woods and sky. I got out of my car and listened. A verse of some sort seemed to be repeating over and over but I couldn't understand what was being said. It sounded like a different language. I got back in my car. It continued. I got out again but still couldn't make out her words. Her voice seemed to come from everywhere, echoing as if afar yet filled the air around me as if close. I got back in my car. I sat for a long time listening to this voice wondering what this might be, who it might be. I thought of the bottle of sedatives again. What about Ashley? What about Dan? But broken dreams, devastation and emptiness had a grip on my soul. I meant nothing. Life meant nothing. I cried and cried, then sat in a state of numbness. The woman's voice continued to echo all around me. I don't know why or even how, but something made me start my car and I made my way back home. I stumbled into our camper that sat in the back yard, lay on the bed and sobbed. I had been unable to protect Leisha or Ashley. My beautiful daughter was gone. How do I exist without her? Everything was destroyed. My reason for being, all that I believed in had been taken away. My husband had seen me pull into the yard so came looking for me. He comforted me as best he could while I shook from exhaustion and sorrow.

The next day I went into the bathroom and closed the door.

This was the only place I could go to get away from my husband's concerned, watchful eye. I closed my eyes and just stood there. A vision of Jesus instantly appeared. Many angels were standing behind him. I was confused at what I had seen. Had I imagined it in my state of desperation? I closed my eyes again but saw nothing. Unaware of anything or anyone, I stumbled through the next two days. I couldn't sleep. I felt sick. My mind and body were numb. While lying in bed at night, another vision appeared to me. It was Jesus again. He was holding Leisha's body in his arms. It took a few seconds to process what I had just seen. Is this real??! Oh, my God! Jesus himself...carried *"my Leisha"*?!! As the implications began to resonate within me, tears flooded my eyes but this time, due to a glimmer of hope. I whispered, "Thank you...thank you...thank you."

Ashley was not doing well. She cried endlessly, telling her father and I that it should have been her. She kept saying, "I'm the sick one, it should have been me! It's not fair!!! I want my sister!!!" We were both worried about her. I began making calls to find a counselor. Ashley agreed to go only if her Dad and I went with her. After speaking to several counselors, I found a woman with grief counseling experience and who also had worked with people who'd had serious illnesses. I provided all of the circumstances affecting Ash. Her comments seemed sincere and compassionate. She provided insight that could have only come from experience, which was crucial. We needed someone who could be effective right away. Time didn't allow for trial and error and equally important, she could be- gin seeing us right away. During our phone consultation, I had asked that she focus on Ashley. We all needed help but Ash needed it most.

Our counselor created a soft, comfortable environment for us to share our pain. Every session began with lighting a candle in Leisha's memory. She allowed each of us the time we needed to express ourselves, even when it seemed words couldn't be found. She asked the right questions to help Ashley understand the confusion, pain and fear that had been thrown at her. Within a four month span, she'd undergone a craniotomy, unsure what the outcome would be, lost her uncle, lost her sister, had a two-year-old child to care for... all at just twenty-four years old. We were all barely holding on. Grief clouds and distorts your judgment. Though the girl's father and I split up many years ago, we still loved our daughters and listening to each other brought perspective and commonality to the loss we shared. Ashley's pain was our pain. The same held true for Ash. Our pain helped her see that she wasn't alone. It helped her recognize we couldn't bear losing her too. It helped her to see that no matter which child we lost, we'd be devastated. It also helped me recognize the impact I would have had on Ashley, had I taken my life that night.

Over the next several months, we met weekly as schedules and weather permitted. Ashley and I began going to dinner together at our favorite Mexican restaurant after each counseling session. We didn't know what to do or how to "be" without Leisha here. Just being in each other's presence helped ease the fear and uncertainty, which for now was all we could hope for.

Today for the first time, I felt energy pulling on my hand when I was reaching for something. Letting the energy move my arm, someone spelled "Love."

Most nights, I'm up for hours typing in my journal on the computer, looking at pictures of Leisha or just sitting and thinking.

One late night, Dan had gone to bed but I couldn't sleep. I sat on the couch trying to focus on a TV show but the ache and burn in my chest was too intense. Physically and emotionally drained, I headed into the spare bedroom to lie down. I'd been lying in bed for a couple of minutes wondering how I was going to find my way and would I ever feel anything other than this pain, when I saw a flash of white light break into the room. Then, as if someone laid something over me, I felt warmth and peace soak into my whole body. It softly melted away the grip of anxiety that had such a tight hold on me. The burning in my neck and chest eased, then stopped. I whispered, "Thank you" and within seconds drifted off to sleep. I cannot aptly describe that beautiful, wondrous moment. I was shown mercy even though I had cursed God. I had done nothing to deserve it, yet he chose to bless me with comfort and the ability to see a glimpse of one of his angels so that I would know it was from Him.

Matthew 5:4: NIV

"Blessed are those who mourn, for they will be comforted."

Isaiah 41:10: NIV

"So do not fear, for I am with you; do not be dismayed, for I am your God. I will strengthen you and help you; I will uphold you with my righteous right hand."

Chapter

Six

❧

Darkness Seeks an Angry Heart

An unguarded door is an open invitation.

Starting with a few people that had come forward, either by email or in person, I began documenting as much information as I could on events that occurred the evening of the accident. As new names surfaced, I reached out to them as well. I was determined to understand every second of that entire evening...where she went, who she talked to, what the conversations were, etc. If I could account for every moment, it might help me understand why this horrible night had occurred. Hearing about certain events was difficult. I wanted to punish anyone that caused Leish even the slightest pain. Once I had exhausted all potential leads, I put all information together in a chronological listing and provided copies to both the DA and civil attorney.

September 7, 2010: The car Leisha was traveling in that evening had flipped at least a couple of times when entering the highway from the on ramp. I contacted the state highway department to determine who was working in the toll booth that evening to see if

they could recall anything that might help us understand what happened. I was told they would check the schedules for that date and get back to me. I requested that once they determine who it was, to have that specific person call me directly. To my surprise, I received a return call that afternoon from the woman who had been working the night of the accident. After expressing her condolences, she told me that she recalled John Doe going through the booth that evening. She remembered him asking to use a bathroom and when told there was none available he became confrontational, which made her pay more attention to details. She also remembered the smell of alcohol so peered into his car. She noticed a person lying still on the front passenger seat with what looked like a blanket or towel covering her. She could see long hair so assumed the person was female. She said she was not moving or talking, just lying there. John Doe fished around for money then sped off after handing it to her. She described his car and the exact T-shirt and the baseball hat that he was wearing backwards that evening. This confirmed for me that she recalled the correct vehicle and passengers. Was Leisha even conscious? Is that why she didn't have her seat belt on?? It wasn't like her not to. She al- ways wore it. A new level of anguish unfolded. All the fears a mother has for her children, wanting to protect them from danger and pain, had come to be. I provided this information to our attorney and the DA. A few days later, I spoke with the coroner that had examined Leisha. After explaining what the toll booth worker had told me, I asked if he remembered anything that would support any injuries that may have been inflicted prior to the accident. Unfortunately, he told me that due to the number and nature of injuries she had sustained in the accident, it would be impossible to distinguish between the two.

September 7, 2010: I felt energy pulling at my hand again. Reaching out, as it had before, it spelled, "Love."

Later that week, I met with the fire chief who provided me with a copy of the run report. He told me that he felt the EMT had followed protocols appropriately, taking correct actions. I disagreed and told him what had been relayed to me by the two CNA's. He again told me he felt the EMT followed protocols appropriately. I told him I'd be in touch then departed. I immediately contacted the state of Maine's Emergency Medical Services, Department of Public Safety. The woman I spoke with explained that if I wanted to proceed with charges, a formal written complaint needed to be submit- ted and that it would be reviewed by the board. Since our attorney was already requesting information on our behalf, I would wait for the results before moving forward.

October, 2010. *It's been nine weeks. Another sleepless night. I've lay awake for the last hour or so thinking of you, watching for you. It's been so long since I've spoken to the physical you, heard your voice or have been able to hug you. I miss you so much. How am I going to get through the months and years ahead? Every day is a struggle and seems endless. What little sleep I do get, allows me to escape for only a short while. I've been listening to a CD that was given to us by our counselor. The songs were written and performed by a woman who lost her daughter to cancer. They speak of her pain but it's as if I had written them myself. Various verses resonate more than others, "There's no power in this pain...." and "It's too early in the morning and too late in my life, to write a different story, to hope for different lines, I guess it's finally hit me what forever really means, that no amount of dreaming will bring you back to me."*

I began receiving phone calls from John Doe's insurance company trying to get information. I also received calls from a firm representing the lender where Leisha had a small loan remaining on a laptop she'd purchased about eighteen months back. She'd missed a couple of payments during the previous year so large penalty fees and interest had begun to accrue. Both Leish and I tried working with them to settle and pay off the loan but they refused to pull back these large fees leaving a balance that was higher than what the lap- top was worth. I passed this information along to an attorney from my home town who was assisting with items outside the realm of the civil proceeding. We'd gone to school together as kids and his family was friends with my girl's father's family. He was compassionate and easy to work with. He handled each item with as little involvement as necessary from us, which was appreciated when faced with so many other responsibilities and challenges. Over the next few months, we were notified that the firm refused to write off the balance of Leisha's loan regardless of the circumstances. We had tried working with these people, who were very rude at times, with no results. The lender holding Leisha's student loans discharged the entire balance due yet this company was demanding payment. I re fused to give them a penny.

Our attorney sent a letter stating "The EMT fell under the city's jurisdiction as an employee and by law, was immune from suit due to the Maine Tort Claims Act. This Act provides that all governmental entities are immune from suit on tort claims seeking recovery of damages and provides that only express statutory exceptions will overcome this immunity from suit. When the court considers a claim of governmental immunity under this Act, immunity is the rule and exceptions to immunity are strictly construed, thus acting as a shield." The job of an EMT is to help those who are hurt and to save lives if possible. I've heard story after story of how EMT's have made a difference by providing heartfelt care and making good decisions that saved lives. Unfortunately, this wasn't our story. I at least wanted to provide a formal complaint to the state in hopes that this didn't happen to someone else's loved one. After several weeks of obtaining information, meeting with our attorney and the fire chief, I had now received copies of all possible documentation regarding the EMT's actions that evening. I had the run report, an incident report, police department logs, a prehospital care report and a written statement from the EMT to the fire chief outlininghis recollection and opinion of the evening's events. From what I read, they supported the information provided by others that were there and trying to help save Leish. I printed a copy of the state's EMT protocols and read through all of them. There were several areas that clearly outlined actions to be taken for patients in critical situations but they were not followed. I compiled all information into a com- plaint, requesting that the EMT's license be revoked. After months of follow up, I finally received a letter of denial. It had become just another layer of debris that lay over me, adding to the weight that had already lodged me into darkness.

A few days later, I received an email from the private investigator. In previous conversations, I had asked that he provide his findings after reading through the DA's and police reports. I was expecting an email summarizing these findings so naively began reading each page. Instead, I found that he had forwarded me a copy of his handwritten notes he'd made while reading through the reports. Though it provided answers to a lot of questions, I was horrified to come upon very descriptive details of Leisha's injuries. Injuries that I'd been unaware of. Thoughts and images of her being in distress flooded my mind. Was she conscious? Did she feel pain?! Pressure gripped my chest and throat so tightly I could barely breathe. My whole body shook. I later called our attorney to let him know what I had been sent, asking for discretion and sensitivity with all future correspondence. He, of course, was apologetic and assured me that he'd relay this to all parties helping on our case. I understand this is routine to them but for those of us on the other end, it's scarring. To this day, I struggle with what she may have felt. It takes all my strength to push those thoughts away.

For the last couple of weeks, every few days or so, energy pulls on my hand and arm spelling, "Love" each time.

I feel as though I have no perspective or control of my life. It's as if a cold, raging river has swept me away, carelessly tossing me about and pulling me under now and then by the strong current. I move along because that's all I can do. Just when I think I can't hold my breath any longer, I'm forced to the surface to face continuation and more unwelcomed challenges. With no time to gain strength or take a deep breath, I'm submerged once more as another sobering task lay before us. A head stone needed to be chosen. Not getting one was out of the question but I dreaded every aspect of doing so. Ashley, her Dad and I found ourselves meeting with a salesman. We were shown various stones, shapes, colors, designs and lettering options. We were asked if we wanted a saying, verse or some other wording engraved, what design did we want, and what should the layout be? I looked at the pictures he offered but anxiety was blocking me from hearing his words or completing a thought. Though he was very polite, the gentleman helping us seemed oblivious to our pain. Didn't he know how hard this was? I tried to understand that it was his job to provide all options. I could see that Ashley was struggling also. Excusing ourselves, I took Ashley's arm and we stepped outside, only to find that we were surrounded by headstones. We just stood there among them, looking from one to the other. Our hearts ached and we both felt sick inside. We hugged, trying to console one another. We had to choose a headstone for our Leisha. It tore at all three of us. We wanted only the best for her but what is "the best" when it comes to buying a headstone for your child? How do you put love into something like that? It was an agonizing decision. It felt as if we had accepted she was gone. It felt final. It felt wrong.

Forcing our way back inside, we looked over a few more options. Ashley wanted cursive style lettering because Leisha wrote in cursive most of the time. Her Dad and I agreed that would be nice. Ash had given Leisha a frame a few years back that had, "Sister's first, friends forever" engraved on it. She asked if these words could be added. Of course we wanted this for her...for them both. A design was chosen and an engraving of "In our hearts and thoughts forever" was requested. As we departed, the salesman promised to email various designs with the options we'd chosen. Over the next few days, the three of us reviewed the sketches, made a final decision and placed our order. Weeks later, the stone was installed. It took several days for me to gather enough courage to go to the cemetery. When I finally got there, seeing her name etched in the stone was insufferable. My heart broke all over again.

November 5, 2010: John Doe is indicted on charges of Manslaughter and Aggravated Criminal OUI. My daughter was taken from us within a moment's time yet it took nearly three months to indict him.

November 10, 2010: *Since they were born, I've prayed for God to keep my girls safe and healthy. Within five months, He seemed to have no regard for either request. Ashley had a brain tumor and Leisha was taken from me in a car accident. It was difficult enough to witness the fear Ashley felt, the invasiveness of her surgery and the uncertainty of her future looming over us. Losing Leish has left me unbalanced, empty and overwhelmed by a constant physical and emotional aching throughout. My girls and I have been there for each other through challenges, heartaches and happy times. I enjoyed watching them grow into beautiful, caring, young women. We created many traditions through the years, which not only produced a multitude of wonderful memories but had a hand in shaping who they were as people along the way. I dread each season as it approaches now. I don't know how to make new memories without Leisha being here to participate in them. She's not here to play her part. She's not here for me to shower her with gifts and love or to share conversations or recipes...or to listen to her dreams. I used to get choked up watching the girls open a gift that I felt was special to them. This year, I'm choking back tears of pain. I miss her so much. It's been 92 days.*

The same familiar energy pulling on my hand today caused it to spell "Love" then "Jesus."

November 17, 2010: I received a letter from our civil attorney today letting us know that there's an issue with the blood test taken the night of the accident. When an accident occurs due to alcohol consumption, the state trooper contacts a special phlebotomist from a list carried with them. Several such specialists were called the night of Leisha's accident but none of them answered the phone. John Doe had to be taken to the hospital where the blood test was administered. The test was not conducted under the direct supervision of the state trooper, however, so a subpoena had to be issued to acquire the blood samples and results, which were now at the State crime lab. John Doe is still denying he was drunk, driving recklessly or acting aggressively towards Leisha.

I barely slept over the next few days. The desperation at times is so overwhelming. During one of the few moments of sleep that did come one evening, I awoke feeling as though someone was touching the right side of my face. I saw a flash of Leisha's face in my mind. I opened my eyes but was unable to see her. I closed my eyes again and saw twinkles then an angel bending down to touch me. She was looking upward while her hands reached towards me.

Isaiah 49:13 NIV
"For the Lord comforts his people and will have compassion on his afflicted ones."

November 20, 2010: I invited several of Leisha's closest friends to our home in remembrance of her for the upcoming holidays. I was apprehensive on whether it would be too emotional for all of us but our time together was comforting. Ashley and I made a stew and some appetizers and we started a fire in the backyard fire pit. I set out all the photo albums that had accumulated over the years for everyone to look through and ran a slide show on the computer containing hundreds of pictures with Leisha in them. Some of the girls and I went upstairs to the spare room to see some of Leisha's things that I now had. They all sat on the bed that's covered with the quilt she had made. I read a couple of entries from her diary to them. Comments were made at how beautifully she wrote and how observant and insightful she was. I went downstairs to interact with some of her other friends for a few minutes before heading back up- stairs. Finding the girls sitting or lying across the bed reminiscing, I was touched that they felt so at home and were genuinely comforted by Leisha's belongings. Bobby later picked up my husband's guitar and started picking away. Soon some of us were singing along. One friend performed "Knocking on Heaven's Door" while another sang "Halo" for us. The music had become a perfect addition to the heart- felt tribute that seem to flow effortlessly. Dusty later mentioned that it was a blue moon that evening. We looked up at the sky to find a halo brightly shining around the moon. Someone stated "Leisha is our angel now." We all silently nodded in agreement.

November 25, 2010: It's Thanksgiving. Our first without her. Ashley and Lexy spent the evening at our house and the three of us shared our king size bed together. I lay there thinking of how Leisha, Ashley and I would sleep together from time to time when they were younger. I yearned for another opportunity to do so. Leisha would have said or done something to make us laugh uncontrollably. We used to laugh so hard that tears would run down our cheeks. After chatting for a while, Leish and Lexy would have fallen asleep, lightly snoring in harmony together. A melody I would have enjoyed.

Ash and I lay there talking only on occasion. Our silence was understood. Just being together was what we both needed. Fuchsia colored energy appeared above us for a short time, swirling and surging in and out. We both saw it at the same time, pointing at the same spot. Leisha? An angel? We didn't know. I felt a touch on my face for a moment. Lexy had fallen asleep. A few minutes later, so did Ashley and at some point, I followed.

Morning came. Keeping busy was the best way to cope and avoid thinking too much. While cleaning up from breakfast though, I felt desperation setting in. I went upstairs to collect myself. After a few tears, I took a long deep breath and rejoined everyone in the kitchen. We forced ourselves into the car and began the drive to my Mom's house for dinner. After everyone was finished eating, I went into the bathroom and shut the door so that I could be alone. It was difficult being around people. I just stood there with my eyes closed. Instantly a strong, fuzzy feeling energy surrounded my hands, arms and face. A vision of Jesus appeared with many angels standing on both sides and behind him. The edges of the angels were blurred and opaque, blending together a bit but I could discern halos, wings and individual shapes. Their arms were outstretched at first, then their hands moved together as though praying. Were they calling me to open myself to their love and light? Who am I to be blessed with such a gift as this? Why me? I've done nothing with my life that deserves such grace and honor. Awe and humbleness flooded through me as I thanked Jesus. I quickly brought Ashley into the room with me and told her what I had just seen. She said, "I get angry with God then I remember that he and Jesus brought Leisha into our lives in the first place." We both closed our eyes and held out our hands. She wasn't able to see the visions I had seen but was instantly able to feel their energy. A few moments later, I opened my eyes to see that both of our arms were moving in the same direction at the same time...outstretched, then inward, repeating several times. Her eyes were still closed. It was just as I had seen the angels doing before Ash had come into the room with me. I closed my eyes again.

I saw nothing further but felt our hands come together and stay there.

Matthew 11:28 NIV

"Come to me, all you who are weary and burdened, and I will give you rest. Take my yoke upon you and learn from me, for I am gentle and humble in heart, and you will find rest for your souls. For my yoke is easy and my burden is light."

November 30, 2010: Over the last couple of years, we'd been casually looking for a new house or ways to expand our existing home. I couldn't bear to leave Leisha's things in storage. Our existing home was too small to accommodate both hers and ours so we began looking again. At the end of November, we found several acres on a small lake. It was perfect. I needed privacy. The woods, water and wildlife had always helped calm and ground me when going through a difficult time. Now more than ever, I needed the serenity that only nature could provide. I was struggling and needed that refuge. We closed on the land in November with plans to put our existing home on the market the following spring.

December 7, 2010: On the way home from work, I felt energy pulling on me. I put my hand out but felt pressure pushing it back towards me. I felt the pressure on my hand lighten and a different energy began pulling on me. It was heavier and strong. The pressure around my hand became very intense and I suddenly felt a shock as if touching an electrical outlet. It hurt. I quickly pulled away. Confusion set in as my hand then spelled "Open door, Open window." I didn't understand at first then realized that "I" was an open door and evil or bad energy had found me. I then realized that someone had tried to keep my hands in close to my body to avoid connecting with this negative, hurtful energy. I kept my hands to myself for the next few days while trying to figure out what had happened and how to handle this new source of energy I had come into contact with.

A new level of confusion and fear cast a shadow over the light that had begun breaking through the despair I'd been immersed in since losing Leisha. I'd lost my daughter, my friend and myself. I needed her. The visions that had been gifted to me were healing and provided that hope that she still existed. A thirst for knowledge of God, Jesus and heaven had begun to grow within me. The darkness and physical discomfort I'd experienced a couple days before now left me apprehensive and hesitant. Was this new encounter evil? How could such negative energy exist simultaneously with Grace from God? This new experience clouded my thinking and heart even further. I didn't know what to do. While sitting at home one afternoon trying to make sense of it all, I felt soft energy touch me. I reached out my right hand. It spelled, "You don't understand. Jesus loves Wanda. Wanda needs God." I began to cry and asked if God thought I was still angry about Leisha's death? "Yes." I said, "I don't know what I feel other than pain, sadness and loss. How can I not feel the loss of my daughter? How can I not grieve?" "Leisha is angel under the Lord." Emotion poured from me. Happiness, pride and sadness all in one. My hand then spelled, "Don't cry. Rejoice." "How? How can I when she's gone?" "Leisha is angel."

1 Peter 5:8 NIV
"Be alert and of sober mind. Your enemy the devil prowls around like a roaring lion looking for someone to devour."

Matthew 10:28 NIV
"Do not be afraid of those who kill the body but cannot kill the soul. Rather, be afraid of the One who can destroy both soul and body in hell."

Chapter

Seven

Searching for Answers

When discouraged and alone, we have a choice…
be frozen by fear or step forward to find shelter.

December 17, 2010: *I found a CD compilation of Christmas songs Leisha had made, titled "Christmas 2009." I listened to it on the way to work, expecting it to be a little too "new age" for my taste. But instead, it was a nice mix of old and new. I felt pride and comfort as I heard song after song. Bing Crosby, Andy Williams, Melissa Etheridge, Rob Thomas and more. They were well chosen, meaningful and warm. One particular favorite is "Mistletoe" sung by Colbie Caillat. Her style sounds fresh and easy, which reminds me of Leish. Another favorite is a duet with Josh Groban and Brian McKnight, titled, "Angels we have heard on high" I listened to it over and over. I miss Leish so much tonight. I want to wrap my arms around her and hug her so tight, never letting go.*

Later that evening, energy pulled at my arm and hand. My hand moved to my heart then spelled out, "Jesus will help you. Must love him." Doesn't he know? "No. Love him. Must love." Have I done something wrong? Is it because my heart still hurts from losing Leisha? "No." Crying now I ask if it's because I'm angry with "John Doe" and the EMT? "Yes. Must forgive." "I don't know if I can." My arm then spells, "Jesus. Must forgive." Nothing more after that. I called Ashley to tell her what I had been told. She said she would never forgive him because he took Leisha from us and ruined our lives and Leisha's life. I told her that God and Jesus have given us an amazing gift with these visions and messages. If Jesus wants us to love and forgive, we need to try. She said Leisha would not forgive if the situation was reversed and one of us had died. I agreed that she would be just as devastated but said, "You keep telling me that you want to be more like her, be more positive, loving and happy. If Leisha was the one here and God, Jesus and the angels were showing us that you were given the honor of being a special enough to be in their presence as she is now, and that God created a place of love and peace for all of us, I know she would be grateful and honored and would try to forgive. She wouldn't let the hate consume her. She never let negativity rule her life. She always found a way to be happy. We need to as well. Leisha is telling us this. Are you going to ignore her? Aren't you going to hear what she wants for us?? Leisha isn't here now. I wish she was but she's not. There's nothing we can do to change that. We need to be grateful for this amazing gift and that Leisha still exists." Ash was crying too hard now to talk. I text her later, "Try to love her as she is now. Let her love you." As I heard myself telling Ashley these words, I knew that I struggled with many of the same feelings she felt. Like Ash, I'm trying to understand what this all means, how to feel and how to move forward without Leish here with us. I'm angry, sad and yet grateful for what is being shown to me.

Christmas is coming. I dread it so much without Leish here. Last year when we took our annual trip to the tree farm to search for a tree, Leish and Ash wondered off with my camera and took pictures. Later that evening when I loaded them, I saw the silly pictures they had taken. Some were pictures of their own shadows and others just of themselves. We giggled about it when I called them. This year, I waited. Thanksgiving came and went and I had no desire to get a tree. The thought of doing so instantly brought anguish and a lump in my throat. I decided that I didn't want to have Christmas at my house. Not this year. I didn't want any of it. No special meal, no music, no holiday movies, no playing games after dinner. Leisha wouldn't be there. Last week, though, it occurred to me that no matter where we go, no matter how we face Christmas, we'd be missing Leisha and the pain would still find us. I also realized that by shutting down all the traditions and special events of the day, I was shutting out Leisha too as if she'd never been part of those traditions. I was running away but reality was there at every turn. It also dawned on me that it would be unfair to Ashley. She's already lost her best friend and sister. Breaking the pattern of those traditions, meant I'd be taking away even more security and normalcy from her. I would be adding to the void. The Sunday before Christmas, we drove to the nearest spot we could find that sold already cut trees and purchased one. I didn't care which one or what it looked like. I just wanted to get it and go home. Ash came over to help decorate the tree and family room. We used Leisha's Christmas decorations, only adding the homemade ornaments Leish and Ash had made for me through the years. Not a year went by without hanging them. It was comforting to have Leisha's things out and appreciate them. They're a reflection of her. Four cone shaped trees wrapped with fuzzy, silver threads were placed on our black stereo cabinet. We draped a white sparkly ribbon she'd kept in and around them. Her light teal, silver and soft purple glass bulbs were hung on the tree. Tears came and went as we unpacked certain items but all were placed out to appreciate what she had chosen and loved. Everything glimmered with softness and warmth. Just like her.

I went to work the next day but couldn't concentrate. The majority of my days since returning after her accident have been the same. I find now that even the simplest tasks are complicated. I sit at my desk sometimes and stare at the monitor trying to comprehend the words that I read over and over. Sometimes I worry that my mind is shutting down completely or that I will remain overwhelmed the rest of my life. Will I ever be able to function at a level other than empty? Will there ever be some kind of "normal" again? I had been spiraling downward at an alarming rate, halted only by the vision of Jesus carrying Leisha to heaven. Despite the comfort this blessing brought, emptiness and sadness remain. I miss her and am struggling to find my way.

December 21, 2010: I tried to finish my Christmas shopping but found myself standing still in the middle of the mall. Watching other young woman her age shopping, laughing and having fun was torturous. Why are they here but Leisha's not? How is it that some people never experience any level of tragedy or hard times and others do? Shopping was out of the question today. I headed home. The night before Christmas Eve, I forced myself to wrap the few gifts I'd managed to buy. They lay in a pile and as I looked at them, all I saw was a pile. Leish and I used to love wrapping gifts. We enjoyed making each one look festive and exciting. We'd make long ribbon curls, adding bows in bunches and adorn each present with a variety of styles and colors. Not this year. Just paper and a bow on each. I rushed through them, eager to be done. Half way through, I broke down. There were no presents for Leisha. How could I have no presents Leisha?! Why wasn't she still with us?!! I struggled through wrapping the rest and went to bed.

Christmas Eve. Leish always went with us to Dan's parent's house for the evening then spent the night with us so she could be at home on Christmas morning. It was hard to face the family party without her. Ashley met us at our house and we rode over together. It was a long night. I tried to keep it together, not wanting to ruin the evening for everyone else, but found it hard to interact. I missed her presence and missed her funny comments that made us all laugh. I asked the normal, how are you, what's new and so on. I saw their mouths moving but heard only muffled replies. The voice in my head overpowered their words. Where is Leisha? Why are we here? Why did this happen? How can it be Christmas? How is everyone functioning? I was surrounded by people but felt alone. Retreating to the bathroom or garage now and then to let the emotion spill over, I'd then collect myself and rejoin the group. I wanted to go home and be alone. Gratefully, my husband recognized I was struggling and ended our visit early.

Christmas Day: The silence from Leisha's absence was deafening. I felt out of place as if being in someone else's home. Nothing felt familiar or right. At some point, we decided to open gifts. Ash handed me one with a gift tag that read, "From Leisha." I opened it slowly, finding a beautiful clear, snowflake shaped crystal with a picture of Leisha etched into it. I held it to me, muffling my cries with my other hand. It was beautiful. I placed it on the tree just in front of a blue light bulb. The glowing light illuminated her image perfectly. I gazed at it often throughout the day. Later in the evening, Ashley and I were in the kitchen. She was sitting at the table and I was standing near the opening between the dining room and kitchen. I looked up and could see an angel. I called to Ash, telling her what I saw, asking if she could see her. She said no but could see twinkles all around me. I saw the angel three different times within a few moments. I received two wonderful gifts that day. One from Ashley that captured her sister's beauty and one from God, sending his angels to help us.

January 9, 2011: Ashley posted the below message to Leisha's Facebook. I'm worried about her. She's lost without Leisha and feels so much pain.

"Miss you so much big sis. I'm so sorry that this happened to someone so sweet and innocent, how could something so bad happen to you. It's not fair and it's not right. My heart is with you wherever you are. I'm not too far behind. Just like when we were growing up, I was always a step behind you but, I WILL catch up to you."

January 12, 2011: The night before we lost Leisha, I had a dream of a very large lion in Ashley's apartment, just sitting and watching us. Today, I had a vision of a horse that was looking back, then another of multiple horses running. Just after, the lion appeared again. In researching their symbolism, horses can represent the driving force that carries you in life as well as strong emotions. A lion can symbolize courage and strength in overcoming difficulties. I hope these messages are just that.

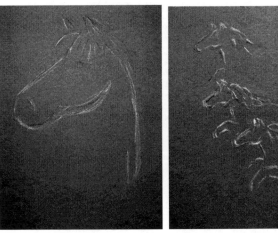

Last night I dreamed I was screaming for Leisha off a very high balcony. No one could hear me. No one was there. Leisha was not there. A few nights later, a very white light shot into my room again. This time I was given a vision of Jesus on the cross. Is the message one of forgiveness and that His death brings life? Life to Leisha? There's so much I don't understand. I thought I did but realize now how unaware I've been. I had just observed the "words" in the bible before without absorbing or conceptualizing. I was too busy thinking of other things the times I did attend church services. Now here I am, unprepared and lost.

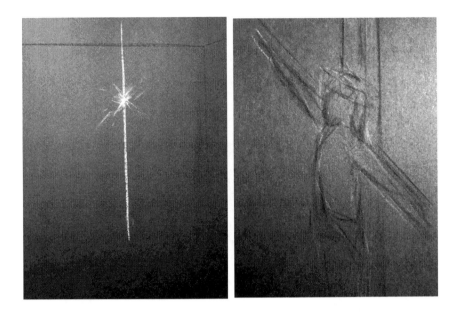

John 11:25 NIV
"Jesus said to her, I am the resurrection and the life. He who believes in me will live, even though he dies."

Ever since I felt that shock in my hand a few weeks ago, there's been negative energy around me. I feel it. I have horrid nightmares and physically feel it pushing on me at times. I wake to slamming noises in the night and have depressive thoughts. A terrible headache has had a grip on me for several weeks now. I have visions of skulls and other symbols of the evil pop into my view while watching television or just sitting and thinking. I feel there's a reason I'm seeing these things, both good and bad. At times, I'm so discouraged and afraid. Other times, I'm so angry. I feel defiant when having intimidating, eerie visions. They only push me towards God. I wonder if God is testing me or whether I'm really being attacked by negative forces. Somedays I feel like I can't deal with this one day longer, then find strength when reading something in the bible that brings comfort or have visions of Jesus, the cross and angels.

Both my girls have had visions off and on through their lives. Today after our counseling session, Ashley text me and said Leisha gave her a message. She said "Mom is sensitive to all the souls around her." My sensitivity and vulnerability allows me to feel all of them, good and not so good. Why would God allow me to see some things and not others? Why does he allow evil to touch us? When will I understand it all?? Leisha must have heard my thoughts because she told Ashley to tell me, "In time."

A few days later, I decided to see if I could find a book to help me understand the visions, the energies, God and Jesus. Someone else must have experienced the same things I have? I went directly to the religious section of a local book store. After finding a new application study bible I began searching for something that might help me understand the spirits and energies I'd been encountering. I found one that explained how faith, love and righteousness are our weapons to fight evil. I brought it home and read it through in just a couple of days. It helped me see that it's as simple as either you have faith or you don't. It's that black and white. God provided a ray of light for me to follow. I feel honored to be offered such a gift when my heart is filled with so much anger, pain and uncertainty. For the first time, I understood what the armor of God meant. I also understood that it's what's in your heart that makes the difference. I want that armor. I want truth.

Ephesians 6:11 NIV
"Put on the full armor of God, so that you can take your stand against

the devil's schemes."

Romans 8:31 NIV
"If God is for us, who can be against us?"

Completely exhausted after too many sleepless nights, I broke down and took a sleeping pill. That evening, Leisha, Dad and my maternal grandmother were spiritually there in a dream. We were all together at my Mom's house on the lake. It was peaceful. They were smiling and led me by the hand. Our cat Raisin that we had lost years ago, was there also just sitting and looking at me. Her fur was shiny, soft and colorful and her eyes were warm. They were all letting me know they were there, watching over me. A bit later in the dream, I noticed the rest of my family sitting around the water as we always do in the summer. Looking out into the cove, I saw a killer whale swimming gracefully. As it surfaced I could see the water shining off its back before diving back under. Everyone was happy, chatting and going about their business as if this were a normal sight. I watched the whale in amazement at how elegant and peaceful it seemed. Then off to the right of the whale, I saw another creature swimming under the water. It swam close to shore and was chasing a large fish, which it finally caught. Then it started to chase another fish. It then turned and tried to bite the whale. I yelled for the whale to watch out. The creature lifted its head out of the water and began snapping at a dog that was amongst us. It then began going after my family members before turning its head towards me, snapping with its tiny, razor sharp teeth. I awoke with a startle. Life, death, rebirth, flow of emotion, good and evil all intertwined. It's an awareness that's becoming more and more tangible. Evil looms even in the most serene settings always waiting to attack. If you're not prepared, that serenity can be ripped away in a moment leaving you with instability, emotional distress and fear. Evil exists and seeks to devour all that it can. I was not prepared for this battle.

I met with my pastor, telling him about the visions and other things that had been happening since Leisha's passing. I also told him about the book I'm reading on deliverance and asked him his thoughts. He helped me to understand the sacrifice Jesus made for all of us. He explained that the cross is symbolic of his sacrifice so that we would all know life after death and the promise of God's kingdom if we accept him as our savior. He also said conversing with or acknowledging in any way the evil spirits, allows them in our lives. If we truly accept Christ as our savior we have no need to worry or acknowledge any of the "shenanigans" of the devil, evil spirits or whatever negative form is there. Keeping God and Jesus in our hearts and lives is how to block and defeat them.

February 11, 2011: I'd had a particularly hard day emotionally. I was supposed to pick my granddaughter up after work to come spend the night with us so her parents could get out for a while but decided to go to their house instead. The kids arrived back at home about 1:00 am and at 1:45 am I was back at my house. My husband had waited up for me but I wanted to try to unwind before going to bed so said goodnight to him as he went on ahead of me. I was exhausted and felt at the edge of breaking. Sitting on the couch, I began to sob uncontrollably. I felt my nose start to run so reached for a napkin. I was surprised to see blood. I kept wiping my nose but the blood came faster. I ran into the bathroom to see what was happening. Grabbing more tissue, I went into our bedroom calling to my husband. He jumped up asking what happened, thinking I had fallen or hit my nose. I told him nothing...it just started to bleed. The stress of losing Leish along with legal matters and worrying about Ashley has been weighing on me. My blood pressure had been rising and was apparently high enough tonight to cause my nose to bleed. Dan held me as I cried and cried. I told him I was so tired of everything! I felt so worn. My nose finally stopped bleeding after a few minutes. He lay awake holding me, watching over me as I drifted off to a much needed sleep.

Two nights after the bloody nose, I awoke feeling my left leg tingling and buzzing from energy that was near. I rolled onto my back watching and waiting to see what was happening. While lying there, a very pure, bright white light began flickering just past the doorway in the next room. It was in front of a stand where pictures of Leisha sit. The flickers of light filled a space of about three feet tall and about one and a half feet wide. It was there for only about ten to fifteen seconds and then gone. I lay awake for a long while hoping to see it again but nothing more. When morning came, I instantly began thinking about the light I had seen that night. Laying there my eyes were closed trying to remember every detail of what I had seen, a vision of Christ on the cross appeared to me. A few moments later a vision of a man appeared who was wearing an off white full length tunic with a dark red cloth draped from his right shoulder down the front and wrapping around to the left. It was Jesus holding a staff. A warm glowing light surrounded Him. He is guiding me.

February 19, 2011: Early in the morning, while standing in my home office, I felt Leisha's presence so strongly. I heard her voice say "Don't stop." I'm so worn, so exhausted mentally, physically and spiritually. She knows I'm struggling just to make it through each day.

A friend of Ashley's passed away just before her surgery took place. Today she told me that he came to her and wanted us both to go to the cemetery where he's buried. I was suspicious of whether it was him saying that or some bad soul playing games with us. We decided to go anyway. Neither of us saw, heard or felt any negative energy while there, which surprised me. I thought about our visit to the cemetery all day, wondering what he wanted us to see. His Mom is very ill. I don't know how she copes. Losing her son and fighting a serious illness must be overwhelmingly difficult. In the middle of the night, I awoke. I lay there still thinking about the day's events and what it all meant when it suddenly came to me. He wanted me to go to the cemetery because he was trying to show me he's gone... like Leisha is. I've been blessed with visions that have helped with the pain and grief. He knew that I could help his mother by telling her about my experiences! Sharing my visions might help lessen her despair. No sooner had the thought come to me when Jesus appeared. He stood with his arms down but reaching out towards me. A soft, glowing white light framed his body with a fuchsia color emanating from within him. It was confirmation that I needed to share my visions with his Mom. Over the next several months, I did just that. I wanted her to see my drawings and hear about the things that I had been experiencing. It helped both of us to talk about our losses. It brought her comfort to know her son lives on, just as Leisha does and to know that God, Jesus and heaven *are real.*

Chapter

Eight

New Challenges

The will of a parent is instinctive and relentless when it comes to the welfare of their children.

February 20, 2011: Two of Leisha's friends were out at a local bar last night and saw John Doe there. He was drinking alcohol. Knowing that he was on probation and not allowed to drink, the police were called. Leisha's friend, Lindsay, had taken her death very hard. Seeing him out drinking instantly infuriated her. Without hesitation, she walked right over and started yelling and throwing punches at him. He punched back, knocking her down. Adrenalin rushing through her, she kicked at him from the floor as the bouncers pulled her away. John Doe left the bar. The police never showed up.

I later found out that the bail conditions form had his date of birth wrong, which is why the dispatcher was unable to find any records. I secured copies of the surveillance videos from the manager of the bar which was provided to the DA. John Doe was arrested for breaking the bail conditions and two weeks later, a judge ruled that he would remain in jail until sentencing on the manslaughter charges that had been brought against him. He'd been seen out at other bars since the accident but no one had been able to prove he was drinking until now. I couldn't understand how he could he be out partying and drinking after causing Leisha's death. She apparently meant absolutely nothing to him. It felt like a slap in the face.

March 4, 2011: Friday morning. Ashley called very upset. Her recent MRI results presented significant changes since the last one a few months earlier. The surgeon wanted to meet with her the following Monday and had told her to bring family. I tried to remain calm but concerned thoughts were racing through my mind also. Was it cancer after all? Did the surgeon not get all the cells and the tumor was still growing? Anxiety poured out of Ash. "I can't do this again! I can't have surgery again, Mom!" Trying to help calm her (and myself) I told her, "We can't jump to conclusions. Let's wait to see what he has to say and go from there. It may be something minor." She replied, "They said it showed significant changes and why would he want family to go with me if it was nothing bad?!" I tried to calm her. "Your Dad and I have gone with you to all of your appointments so they were probably just mentioning it." She acknowledged my comments but I could tell she didn't believe me. After such a horrific year, secretly neither of us were confident it would be anything simple. I called her later in the day and asked that she come spend the day and night with me on Saturday. When

Saturday arrived, we went out for a nice dinner then tried to watch a movie back at home but Ash was too overwhelmed. She just wanted to sleep. We lay in bed chatting for a few moments. As it had done before at Thanks- giving, both of us saw a magenta colored energy appear above her. It moved towards me a bit then back over her. I hoped that it was a healing angel sent to watch over her. On Sunday, I was overwhelmed myself all day. What was happening? Why were all these horrible things happening to us? Hadn't we been through enough? It was a long day and night, waiting and wondering. Very early Monday morning, my maternal grandfather appeared to me. I haven't seen him since just after his passing in 1980. He stood there looking at me for just a few seconds then he showed me the word "superficial." Was he trying to tell me it was nothing major...something little? Was he trying to reassure me? I hoped that his message to me was true.

Later that morning, the neurosurgeon told us that the type of tumor she had, though likely to grow back, is not an aggressively growing type so was unsure why he was seeing such significant changes within months of her surgery. Ashley's last EEG was negative for seizure activity so she had begun weaning off the seizure medication. With that, she'd begun to have slight signs of seizures again. He thought perhaps the MRI could have captured some seizure activity. He ordered another MRI and asked that we schedule another EEG with her neurologist. If no changes in the MRI, he warned us that surgery may be needed again. During the next two weeks, her seizures became more active. Testing and medication adjustments were underway but I felt it was time for a second opinion. After re- searching doctors, facilities and getting input from others that have had similar experiences, we decided on the Brain Tumor Center at Massachusetts General Hospital in Boston. I set up appointments to get testing and consultations underway. Ashley, her Dad and I met with the doctor. Instead of feeling hopeful after our meeting, we all left feeling discouraged. She confirmed what Ashley's current neurosurgeon had stated, which is that it's difficult to find and remove all the tumor cells so many people with astrocytoma, low grade glioma tumors require multiple surgeries throughout their lives. My question to them was, "How much brain tissue can you continue to remove? At some point, it's bound to impact her quality of life, right?" Her reply provided no comfort. If the tumor cells are not removed, they can turn cancerous over time. Our options are to leave them and take that risk of having them turn cancerous or have surgery to remove affected tissue. Depending on the location and number of surgeries, people can lose various functionalities. As discussions came to a close, a functional MRI was ordered. With this type of MRI, Ashley would be asked to blink, move certain parts of her body or speak while testing was underway. This helps them gauge where the tumor cells or questionable tissue is and what impact, if any, it's currently having on her functionality. Once the results were in, the doctor would meet with a panel of medical staff to review the findings and determine next steps.

March 8, 2011: The DA contacted me today letting me know that he'd received a copy of John Doe's medical records from the night of the accident. The impression of two doctors that examined him was that he was intoxicated. He's now looking to get a copy of the blood test but warned us that the opposing attorney was trying to suppress that as evidence.

March 26, 2011: I dreamed of a young boy with blond hair and fair skin. Looking directly at me he kept saying, "Write it down. Write it down. Write it down." The last time he said it very slowly so that I could absorb his words. The messenger in my dream was telling me to take time to document all that I'm experiencing. I had been but sporadically. With this message, I would begin taking time to do so more often.

April 1, 2011: I was praying and asking for direction for Ashley when I received a vision of Mother Mary. I then saw Jesus carrying Ashley. He was there to receive Leisha and take her to Him and now He's showing me that He also carries us when we need His help. He's carrying Ashley through this horrible time. Whether the outcome is good or not so good it's comforting to know that Jesus is there helping her through this.

April 15, 2011: Leisha's birthday is today. She would have been twenty-eight. It's been eight very long months.

I've been studying the bible, watching any religious movie I could find and reading books about people having life after death experiences. A hunger for knowledge has been growing more steadily within me to learn all that I could about God and Jesus. I also began meeting with my pastor about getting baptized. We had several discussions and I read through some literature he'd given me. I learned that baptism is symbolic of our commitment and unity with Jesus. We end our old way of thinking and are reborn into a new life with Christ. This is what I wanted so completed the study materials and made plans to be baptized along with five others from our congregation. When the day arrived, we waited in the stairway that led to the baptismal pool. The mother of a teenager being baptized waited with us as well as another woman who was helping direct us. They both knew of my loss and the health issues Ashley is facing. In talking with one of them, she told me she'd just lost her husband this past winter. She said she had never seen angels or twinkles be- fore but since her husband passed away, she now does. I was the first person she'd met who also sees them. It helped her know it was good and there were others who had the same experience. Pastor Howe walked down the stairs on the other side of the baptismal pool, entering the water. I became overwhelmed with emotion. He's such a wonderful, kind and spiritual man. His part in our baptism made it all the more sincere and blessed. I covered my face with a washcloth I had brought with me to muffle the sobs that suddenly emerged. The other mother waiting with her daughter reached over and hugged me. She said, I understand. As she pointed to the first three birth stones on her mother's ring, she said, "I've lost these three." My heart broke for her. I couldn't begin to understand the amount of grief and pain she must have gone through. We think we're all alone when we're suffering but people all around us are going through difficult times also. Some more than others. It helped to be given this awareness.

April 24, 2011: Easter had always been such a fun day for us by sharing a special meal, presents and egg hunts. Last year we had dinner at Ashley's apartment because she had just had surgery. Leisha helped me cook dinner and hide plastic eggs filled with treats for Lexy. Leish and I acted so surprised as Lexy found each egg. We soaked in the excitement and wonder shining in her little face. This year felt so empty without Leish. We had a small dinner at our house and hid some eggs in the yard for Lexy to find but nothing more. That evening when lying in bed, I had visions of angels. One of them had long dark hair and very large wings. She was beautiful.

April 29, 2011: Last night I awoke at 3:45 am and could hear someone saying, "Dissertation" over and over. I couldn't see anyone in my room. I just heard a man's voice. It was clearly another message for me to document my experiences so I could write this book.

May 8, 2011: Mother's Day. Ashley and I met at the cemetery to plant flowers for Leisha. I struggled with composure, trying to breathe through the sadness. The sadness evolved into anger. I quickened my pace as an attempt to avoid the emotions that I was quickly losing control of. Planting flowers at my daughter's grave site on Mother's Day is not supposed to happen!! Why isn't Leisha here with us so we could have a beautiful, fun day together like we've always done in the past? When the flowers had been planted, we stood back to observe. Ashley broke down. I held her and we stood together letting our sorrow pour out. It helped to be together. After a short time, we departed, meeting back at my house. My granddaughter brought a spark of light and warmth that we all needed. She's so easy going, happy, sweet and full of energy. When first learning to talk, she was unable to say Auntie Leisha. It came out as Ya Ya, so Ya Ya she became. She loved Leish and Leish loved her. Leisha was so proud to be an Auntie. She spent every minute she could with her little niece. Lexy keeps asking us, "Where's Ya Ya?" When she gets upset about something she cries and tells us, "I want my Ya Ya." Before packing up Leisha's apartment, Ash, Lexy and I went over for one last time. When we opened the front door, Lexy ran in all excited yelling for Ya Ya. It broke our hearts. She doesn't understand why her Ya Ya is suddenly gone.

The day pushed on and Ashley headed home. The pain I'd been suppressing during Leisha's birthday, Easter and now Mother's Day began breaking through. I needed to get out of the house so went for a ride but just a short distance away I had to pull into a parking lot. I was no longer able to, nor wanted to hold it in. Emotion erupted from me. I had no control. I told God, it was all too much for me losing Leisha, Pete and Cookie. Ashley is possibly still sick and her future is uncertain. It weighs on me all the time. What will I do if I lose her too?! The spirits of those that have passed want to talk to me all the time. Though some seem as though they're just lost, some are mean, feeling evil and cold. It's all too much! I cried out, "I'm grateful for Jesus bringing Leisha to heaven, for the visions, for everything...but I miss her!!!! I want her back!!!" My hands covered my face as I sobbed uncontrollably. I began to hyperventilate. Trying to slow my breathing and calm down, I closed my eyes. I began to see swirling blue and white energy like wisps of smoke meeting to embrace and then swirl into a beautifully shaped ball, with tiny white sparkles dancing within. This happened several times before resting directly in front of my focus. I was amazed at how tangible it appeared, as if physically there and able to touch it. The energy began to float up and over to the right of my view. Then I saw Leisha as an angel. Her arms were positioned as if holding something...someone...me. I watched her for a few moments, then I saw a man's profile appear just above and to the right. I could only see the outline of his face. He was looking at Leisha. The outline of his face was milky white and clear at the same time. No hair, no beard...not Jesus. Who was it? Was this God creating himself in an image I could understand?!! There are no words to describe how beautiful and amazing this was. I feel so honored and humbled that "I" have been allowed this gift. Leisha "is."

She's safe and continues to be! Thank you, God! Thank you, Jesus!

Deuteronomy 10:21 NIV
"He is the one you praise; he is your God, who performed for you those great and awesome wonders you saw with your own eyes."

June 13, 2011: After trying for some time, I was finally able to meet with two friends of Leisha's who were with her just before the accident that evening. They told me that they were standing outside of a pizza place when Leish came walking down the sidewalk and began chatting with them. They provided details on their conversations and said that John Doe began calling her cell phone and yelling at her. They said she invited him to join them for pizza, telling him where they were but he kept hanging up on her. They then shared details on John Doe's rude and aggressive behavior toward Leish when he pulled up in front of the pizza place. Their testimonies sup- ported that of the police officer that had earlier told Leisha's friend what he had observed. Anger, rudeness and aggression. One of the young men told me that he tried to get Leish to not go with John Doe but she told him that she'd be ok. I thanked them both for their friendship, help and willingness to provide statements which helped support John Doe's aggressive, unfounded behavior that night.

June 24, 2011: I had an intense dream last night, where a man was screaming with pain and agony. I turned to see what was happening and saw him lying on the ground. As I watched, every bit of flesh, muscle and all his organs bubbled and melted away as if acid had been poured on him. After just moments, all that remained was a skeleton but his heart was still beating within his ribcage. The message I got from this is that our physical bodies are subject to pain, sickness and affliction but our souls, can never die. Our hearts reveal who we are, whether good or bad. This dream made me wonder what my heart reveals to Jesus? Just after I awoke, a lion appeared to me at two different moments, the latter of which he was roaring with his mouth open very wide. The saying, "To have the heart of a lion" immediately came to mind. I've always felt that I was an honest, caring person with integrity and solid direction but I'm learning that the standards I created through my life were my standards, not God's. It's easy to think that we can be loving, compassionate and forgiving at all times but it's not as easy as it sounds no matter how good our intentions are. Our egos are forever getting in the way. We have fears, expectations and ideals that we place importance on but we're never prepared for someone taking the life of our child. The foundation I had built, though based on solid principles, was not strong enough to bring me through this loss. The more I study the bible, the more I realize that I had created filters on how life should be lived and how people should be. They're all filters that suited my expectations, not God's. I need the heart of a lion...the heart of Jesus.

The last few months have been stressful as we've worked with doctors to determine Ashley's condition. I worked with her current neurosurgeon and the hospital where she had her surgery to have all documentation sent to the Brain Tumor Center in Boston. Additional MRI's were ordered, the old biopsy results reviewed, new ones completed from the original tissue taken during surgery last year and meetings with neurologists and surgeons have been held. While awaiting the results of all the new tests, adjustments have been made to her medications. A new milder anxiety medication was introduced as they weaned her off the 2,000 mgs of Kepra that she'd been taking each day. Ash had developed intense migraines so a new medication was introduced to help. Unfortunately, the wrong dosage was prescribed by her neurologist (separate from her neurosurgeon) causing Ashley severe head pain, confusion and a spike in blood pressure. He wasn't taking Ashley's calls seriously so I contacted his office myself. Being met with the same, "we're busy and will call you when we have time" routine, I left some strongly worded messages on their voice messaging system. Meanwhile, I placed a call to her primary care physician, who set up an immediate appointment. On our way there, we got a call from the neurologist's assistant. I let her know that we were heading to see her primary care doctor and they had requested she contact them to provide recent physician notes. Ashley carried the migraine prescription with her because her headaches were so bad. After looking at the prescription, her primary doctor noticed they had prescribed way too much medication which was causing her blood vessels to severely constrict. They told her to stop the medication immediately, letting us know that she was close to "over dosing." If we hadn't gone to see this doctor, she could have endured more severe consequences, including death!! Really???!!! When do the challenges and incompetency's end?! I immediately provided this information to her neurologist's office and demanded a new doctor be assigned. As much as I wanted to file some kind of action against this doctor, I just didn't have it in me. We depend on all the various professions to help us when needed and too many of them have let us down.

July 29, 2011: After nearly four long months since her last MRI, surgery has been put on hold!! The doctors are confident that the changes shown in the images are due to scar tissue finally showing up. They will continue to monitor her with additional MRI's every three months. If any additional changes appear, we'll meet to determine next steps. If none, we keep moving forward with the hope that all tumor cells were removed and no more surgeries will be needed. With much of the medication out of her system now, relieved that another surgery is not the direction and fall classes about to begin, she's feeling better than she has in nearly two years. What a tremendous weight lifted off her shoulders and mine. I cannot de- scribe the strain of grieving for one daughter and worrying that I might lose the other too. For now, a reprieve...at last. My grandfather was right. It was "superficial" scar tissue.

August 15, 2011: The one-year anniversary was approaching. I wanted to have some type of gathering in Leisha's honor, but felt overwhelmed and didn't know how to go about it. Thankfully Leisha's friend, Lindsay, stepped in to help by reserving a room at a local restaurant and sending out the communications. Many of Leisha's friends attended. I was touched by how fresh her presence still is in their lives and hearts. She was... and is... so loved. A lot of stories and fun memories were shared. We placed pictures of Leish all around for everyone to enjoy and to help bring her presence to each of us this evening. Another friend of Leisha's wrote and recorded a song about her. His lyrics and soft rock music captured the very essence of her while complimenting her personality.

"Don't Worry"

Music and Lyrics by Todd Orcutt Copyright © 2011 All rights reserved

In memory of Leisha Alura Tarbox

Verse
I can't believe it, the night she died,
She was only 27 and had the rest of her life
To get married, have a baby, raise a child of her own
She loved her little baby niece, longed to see her grow
She was a beauty, had the smile of a child
She was a wild one, no one could tame her style
She was a daughter, a sister, apple of your eye
She would never want to see us cry

Chorus
She was so loved, loved, loved
Sunshine in the sky above
She says Don't worry baby
It will be all right
I'll be waiting on the other side

She was the lady all the girls want to be
A flash of lightning, the life of the party
She loved her family and her friends
Her laugh made them smile

She always glowed in pictures, she was a beautiful child
She is the reason, we cried yesterday
The hole in our lives, leaves an empty space
At her graveside, everyone gathered around
And we tried to lay our burden down

Chorus

She was so loved, loved,loved
Sunshine in the sky above
She says, Don't worry baby
It will be all right
I'll be waiting on the other side

Verse
Well you can drown, in your sorrow
Or find some joy, and live for tomorrow
If she was here right now she'd smile and show us how
To laugh, smile and go on even though she's gone
There is no reason, no what ifs or whys
It does not make sense, but we have to survive
She gave us lifetimes full of memories
Left an impression on you and me

Chorus
She was so loved, loved,loved
Sunshine in the sky above
She says, Don't worry baby
It will be all right
I'll be waiting on the other side

She says, Now don't worry baby

It will be all right
I'll be waiting on the other side

Chapter

Nine

❧

Contemplation

*To thoughtfully consider something for a long time.
To deliberate and reflect on all the facts.*

Our house sold in August 2011. We wanted to build a bigger, more open concept home so that we could incorporate Leisha's things in with ours. A hurricane just happened to find its way to our area the weekend before closing, which of course was when we planned to move. To make things even more interesting, we lost power for three of the four moving days. Nonetheless, most of our belongings were placed in storage. We brought only the bare essentials with us to a very small apartment we'd be renting while waiting for our new house to be built. Finding a short-term rental was challenging. We were happy to finally discover a duplex located in a convenient area for traveling to work, yet close to where the house was being built. It was an adjustment to go from having a house with conveniences and plenty of space to a 700 square foot apartment with only two phone booth sized closets. Our neighbors in the adjoining apartment are very nice, but are also very young. They work late into the night and like to enjoy their surround-sound entertainment system when they get home, which of course is when we're in bed trying to sleep. They also have a small dog that leaves doggy surprises for us to find as we cross the yard to get to our vehicles. Night before last, the kitchen drain pipe let go and water went everywhere when draining the sink after doing dishes. Then last night, our washing machine broke down. It's going to be a long winter...

During July and August, two court hearings were held. It was hard to see John Doe that first time. I stared at him trying to will the emptiness within me to his heart. I want to hear him say, "I'm sorry." I want desperately to see remorse but I've not heard nor seen any evidence of guilt or of being accountable. He must have felt the intensity I was directing at him because he glanced at me a few times. The "Motion to Suppress Evidence" hearing was more difficult to experience. Each person to take the stand is kept out of the court room while the others are being questioned. The state trooper was the first to be questioned. Attempts by the opposing attorney to discredit him were futile. He questioned him over and over asking the same things but from varying angles. The officer handled himself very well, providing honest and professional responses that demonstrated a confident recollection of the evening in question. Our DA followed by asking clarifying questions. John Doe's friends were questioned next, with conflicting statements made. His father then took the stand. He painted his son as an upstanding young man. As a parent, I could appreciate that he would support his child. We love our children, overlook their faults and stand by them when in trouble. But we should also hold them accountable when they're wrong. Some of his statements conflicted with facts and documentation already in hand. He then explained, with a very concerned tone and expression, that his son was arrested and led out of the hospital with no shoes on his feet. I was appalled that he had the nerve to make such a callous statement. All he got was a cut on one of his toes and a few bruises during the accident and he felt bad because he had no shoes to wear??!! His son's reckless and hostile behavior caused such severe trauma to my daughter that she lost her life!! It took an enormous amount of energy to stay seated and remain quiet. I wanted to scream out what it was like to see my daughter in the back room of a funeral home, disfigured from the injuries he caused! He still had his son! It was difficult to sit silently, listening to the details of the accident, what "John Doe" did and didn't say or do, was the blood drawn correctly for the alcohol level test, twisting of truths…on and on and on. His blood alcohol level was twenty-four, which is three times the legal limit. Why couldn't he just admit he was drinking and speeding?

I prepared myself for the evidence of the blood alcohol test to be suppressed. Nothing had been in our favor thus far, why would this be any different. The laws I've encountered seemed to be designed to protect everyone except the innocent, so at this point I wasn't optimistic that the judge's ruling would have a positive outcome. Leisha had not been protected on any level before or since the accident. When I got the call from the DA's office telling me that the judge denied the motion to suppress evidence, I was very surprised. I thanked God for this small victory and relief from sustaining yet another defeating blow. We would press on to establish a credible chain of custody. If we're successful, John Doe may choose to plea bargain. If so, we decide if his terms will be acceptable. If not, we can insist on a trial by jury. The risk with that choice is that the whole jury has to agree or his sentence may be less than what the judge would have imposed during the plea bargain. Why does the person who treated my daughter so horribly, taking her life, get to choose the direction of how the proceedings would go? How does any parent or loved one come to acceptable terms for retribution when the life of their child has been lost at the hands of another? This process is overwhelming, frustrating and at many a turn, unfair. I want it to end and be behind us.

September 22, 2011: After getting into bed for the evening, I was lying there thinking of the day when a vision of horns and eyes appeared. It was very dark around them. I then saw stairs leading down, then saw Leisha as she looked at the funeral home. With- out hesitation, I spit out the words, "Not even close! Jesus already showed me she's in heaven!" I abruptly rolled over and ignored its presence. Sometime later, I fell asleep and dreamed of what looked like a bull in a field. The colors of the bull and the surroundings were brown and black. The next night, I awoke at 3:00 am feeling strong energy. It was the same red energy that had also been making me feel uneasy and anxious lately. Then a brown head with horns appeared. All I could see were the eyes, horns and top of the head. The head and background were again dark brown and black. It felt so uncomfortable, intense and eerie. The red energy flashed again.

I began to pray for strength, courage and protection. Just moments later, blue energy bolted into the room. From the top, the blue light pounded down on the red energy, pushing it to the lower left of my view until it disappeared. I saw nothing for a moment or two then a flash of pure white light shot up to the right and was gone. I couldn't believe what I had just observed! An angel of God fought on *my* behalf. For this to happen, the evil being must have been dangerous. I can only imagine the power of God, Jesus and their army of angels!! So wonderfully amazing!!!!

September 30, 2011: I spoke with the DA today. John Doe's attorney is now trying to discredit the results of the blood test. He's contesting the validity stating protocols were not followed correctly when administering the blood test, thus trying to demonstrate that effective chain of custody had not been established. He also communicated that John Doe continues to claim he had not been drinking alcohol nor had he been speeding. It's so upsetting that he won't take responsibility.

November 28, 2011: Lying in bed at night, I could see light shining down towards me from the upper right side. I also had a vision of a roaring lion.

Dec 2011: I had a vision of a man with long hair and a beard. He had a shawl of some sort draped over his head. I don't know who he was but his presence felt comforting.

December 8, 2011: I had a vision where I was looking upwards and could see a cone shaped tunnel. It was wider at the bottom and the top was narrow. The sides were made up of people and angels all appearing in blue and white colors. At the very top, was a small circle filled with a radiant white light that was moving slightly about, like a flame on a candle when it flickers. The light was more brilliant than any light I have ever seen. Was this God? Was it Jesus? Is His light so intense that I could only bear a small glimpse? I feel that it was a path to heaven lined with angels and beautiful souls. Even to this day, warmth and peace fill my heart when I think of this moment. This one little paragraph cannot justly portray how holy, pure and beyond measure that moment was.

All these years I knew that Jesus existed but never really knew Him. Despite my anger, frustration and confusion, he's returned only love and patience. When seeking answers, they seem to just lift off the pages of a bible passage I decided to read or are pro- vided within a conversation on a Christian talk show I just happen to turn on. The words, *"Let those who have eyes see and those who have ears hear"* come to mind. I really was deaf and blind before. Sitting here at the computer, I began to wonder how Jesus can watch over so many with such an equal level of love? There are so many others in the world that deserve his love much more than I do. As I was considering the enormity of how he sees and loves all, an energy appeared between myself and the monitor. It was white at first, then blue with white twinkles appearing within. I watched as the energy and twinkles surged and began circling, becoming stronger and more visual. The twinkles then spread out within a space of about a foot, being a bit longer than wide. I put my hand out to touch it. My hand lingered there for a moment before I felt soft energy move it to my chest then up to my right side. Movement of my hand spelled, "Jesus loves many." My hand then rose up, then back down and across my key board before quickly shooting straight up to the right and over my head. It was acknowledgment of me beginning to understand the depth of Jesus. It was also another message to write down all that I'm experiencing. I whispered, "Thank you!"

December 12, 2011: I awoke in the night to find an angel standing beside my bed. He or she had fairly short blondish, brown hair. I couldn't see any facial features but could see wings, clothing and hair. This angel only lingered for a few seconds. I watched and waited but saw nothing more.

After a while, I fell back to sleep only to awake again at 4:00 am. Standing beside my bed was another angel. Like all the other angels, I didn't see any facial features but could see her long dark hair and wings very clearly. She too was on the left side of my bed, looking down at me.

December 20, 2011: Our attorney was able to secure copies of surveillance videos from one of the night clubs that both Leisha and John Doe visited the evening of the accident. I watched them over and over and over searching for the missing pieces that remained. Three key events were revealed. One clip shows John Doe entertaining some girl other than my daughter for quite some time, buying beers while doing so. Another clip then shows the two of them leaving the bar together. In another area of the night club, a camera captured Leisha walking by. She was by herself and carrying her teal colored purse. She was friends with some of the staff so I assume stayed and talked with them until quite late because the last clip showed her going down the wooden walkway when exiting the same bar at the end of the evening. She was alone and appeared to be reading or sending a text message. These were her final steps before crossing the street to the pizza place where John Doe inflicts his unfounded anger towards her. I wanted to scream out a warning to her. "Stop!! Don't go, Leish!!" She did nothing to warrant his aggression. "He" hit on another girl. "He" left with that other girl then later treated Leisha disrespectfully. Minutes later she would be gone.

December 25, 2011: No tree this year. I didn't want one. We went to Ashley's apartment to open gifts and spend a little time with them. Ashley put together a book for me that she'd created on line containing many pictures of Leisha. It was beautifully arranged, with thoughtful comments written by many of the pictures. My favorite picture is the one of the word "Love" that Leisha had written in the sand with her toe while at the beach one day. Ashley wrote, "She left love on this Earth" next to this picture. A perfect portrayal of Leisha.

January 17, 2012: I spent a good portion of the morning going back and forth between the DA's office and the state police discussing the status of the blood test. It's been four months since this issue was brought to light and nothing has been resolved. There are limited timeframes established for each portion of this horrific process and time was running out. It started seventeen months ago with filing charges, then waiting for a court date so John Doe could present his plea. He of course pleaded "not guilty." Then there was the discovery period. Then the motion to suppress evidence phase presented itself. Though the motion was denied, John Doe's attorney then made claim against the validity of the blood test. Month after month goes by with no results to prove this claim false. Leisha was taken from us in an instant with no warning yet here we are dealing with red tape and delays week after week, month after month. I was tired of "the process" being an excuse for delayed results. I was also tired of feeling like Leish was a routine traffic violation or some other trivial infraction. I had secured written testimonies from her friends stating how horribly he'd treated her and how he sped away that evening. We have surveillance videos showing him drinking beer. We had several other items of proof that supported both of these behaviors. Having him get off on a technicality such as not establishing chain of custody was NOT an option. During my last conversation with the DA today, a promise was given to apply pressure in removing the obstacles that had been holding up results. Within a couple of days, the he was finally able to secure necessary photographs of the blood vials. These photographs provided the nurses initials and other pertinent information needed to schedule a meeting with hospital personnel. In cases involving alcohol related deaths, following defined protocols while administering the blood test is critical. The meeting successfully provided the appropriate documentation needed to establish a proper chain of custody. One of the nurses that assisted in the blood draw that evening was part of this meeting. She communicated to the DA her recollection of John Doe being unsteady on his feet and smelling of alcohol.

February 21, 2012: For months, I had been trying to find someone to fix Leisha's phone. The front screen had been broken in the accident. I had also contacted her phone carrier to see if they might have records of text messages but no luck. During one of the last court hearings, Leisha's cousin told me about a friend of his that fixed a variety of electronic devices so I stopped by his shop to see if he might be able to help. After a few diagnostics, he determined that all it needed was a new display screen. A week later the new screen was installed and we were able to turn her phone on. I could read what she had read. I could see what she had sent to her friends and look at pictures she'd taken with her phone. It was such a gift to have this insight into her life. I was also, however, able to see the exchanging of text messages between Leish and John Doe, all of which supported his disrespectful treatment of her. I typed them up and sent them to the DA. He immediately contacted me asking that I bring her phone to the state trooper's sergeant. He would be able to create an official record of these text messages which would be admissible in court. A couple of weeks later, we had them as official records and her phone was returned to me.

Chapter

Ten

A New Perspective Unfolds

Clear away the noise so the truth can be revealed.

February 26, 2012: Our new home is finally finished and we're ready to move in. We took a week off from work, rented a moving truck and had the apartment and both rental units emptied in the first two days. It was wonderful to be in our own space again. It felt comforting to have Leisha's things around us also. It's been a long six months waiting for the house to be built but we made it. The water, trees and nature that surround us is so comforting. I took a few moments to stand outside, soak in the peaceful serenity and give thanks to God for this gift.

March 1, 2012: While standing in our bathroom today, I saw a very large ball of pink energy with blue twinkles surging throughout it. Everything in this room is white, including the walls, so it was easy to see the pink energy. I later saw Jesus standing with light all around him. He was wearing a long white tunic.

March 31, 2012: I awoke in the night feeling energy buzzing over my entire body. Being startled from sleep, my first reaction was that it was someone bad. But then, I saw Jesus on the cross. I could see him more clearly than any other time before. At first, the vision of him appeared so that he was close to me. I could see his arms and shoulders and chest. His head was tilted forward, but the de- tails of his face hidden from my view. I could also see the thickness of the wooden cross. The vision then shifted and he appeared further away. An angel then came into view, who was blowing on a long trumpet. Then I saw a big five pointed star, with four smaller stars lined up in a row appearing next. The five-pointed star represents the Star of Bethlehem and Jesus' birth and incarnation. Stars also represent knowledge of good and truth as well as distinguish between light and darkness. Jesus is our light, our salvation. He is the truth and the life.

Revelation 11:15 NIV
"The seventh angel sounded his trumpet, and there were loud voices in heaven, which said:
"The kingdom of the world has become the kingdom of our Lord and of his Messiah, and he will reign for ever and ever."

Ephesians 5:8 NIV
"For you were once darkness, but now you are light in the Lord. Live

as children of light."

A few nights later, I awoke in the night to find the soul of a person leaning over my bed watching me. Their entire body had been burned. It startled me so I jumped up which caused them to disappear from my view. I thought about this poor person all the next day, feeling horrible knowing what pain they must have suffered. Why were they in my room? Were they lost? Hoping they were still nearby, I decided to try talking to them that evening. I called to them and told them how sorry I was that they had died. I told them that they should go to Jesus, that he was loving and kind and that he'd bring them peace. I told them about my brother in law and my daughter and that Jesus and the angels had shown themselves to me so I know they're real. I then said that I'd pray for them. I closed my eyes and began saying the Lord's Prayer. After just a few words though, I had a vision of a fireman. I could only see him from the shoulders up. He was wearing a helmet and gas mask...validation of how this person had died. The vision I'd had wasn't a horrid looking ghost or goblin as they depict in the movies, but a human being that had suffered a tragic death by fire. Jesus then appeared. He was facing me and holding a body in his arms. He slowly turned to His right and began to move away. A woman's face then appeared. She was healed and healthy looking! The person that was burned was a woman. She looked to be between 40 and 50 years old, of medium build and had brownish shoulder length hair. She'd gone to Jesus and he healed her, making her whole! Jesus showed me how he saves us, take us to Him. I'm at such a loss for words to describe what I feel I. I'm truly overwhelmed by His love and majesty. Jesus has given us such a glorious and holy gift. I'm so honored to be al- lowed these visions, the messages they provide and the healing and peace it's providing me. I now know with all my heart that He is our Lord and savior. It brings me to tears...tears of joy that erupts from deep within me. He *is* the way.

John 14:6 NIV
"Jesus answered, "I am the way and the truth and the life. No one comes to the Father except through me."

April 2, 2012: I awoke early in the morning to see a demonic type being walking away from me. Its back was bony and it had scrawny, scraggly wings that had no feathers...just flesh covered bones. It was bald and small. Satan sent his minion to spy on me but he was met with defeat. My heart is wholly given to Jesus and God now. This minion knew he had no power so walked away.

Proverbs 3:5-6 NIV
"Trust in the Lord with all your heart and lean not on your own understanding; in all your ways submit to him, and he will make your paths straight."

May 7, 2012: Dan had sleep apnea surgery two days ago. Today, we went outside for a short walk down to the lake and he suddenly couldn't breathe. He coughed and choked unable to breathe for a minute or so before finally catching his breath. It was scary for both of us. We headed back to the house so he could sit and rest. I kept a close eye on him the remainder of the day. Lots of white and blue twinkles were around him nearly every time I looked over. Angels are watching over him.

May 9, 2012: Final sentencing is today. The judge opened

with an overview, depicting his understanding of the case so far, how the process works and what possible outcomes may occur today. Both attorneys presented their arguments, addressing all parties involved including families and friends that were present. Leisha's Dad, Ashley and I were then allowed to address the judge and speak on Leisha's behalf. Her Dad spoke of how much we loved her and how hard it is without her in our lives now. His words painted a vivid picture of her beauty and ambitions and brought her caring nature to light. Emotion spilled from him as he spoke of how he longs to hear one of her nonchalant comments that always made him laugh. He explained how she could put a positive and humorous spin on any ordinary situation that would otherwise be lost within the routine of life's day to day activities. He misses watching her play with her niece whom she adored. He spoke of her devotion and love for her sister, Ashley, and how she never left her side during her brain surgery or the weeks of recovery that followed. Having to pause to gain composure, he described how hard it is to get through a day without thinking of the loss over and over.

Ashley was too emotional to speak but stood by my side and held two pictures of Leisha for the judge to see as I read the below statement:

We've been going through this process for 21 months now, discussing "John Doe", "his" denial, "his" short comings, how "he" feels and what "he's" saying, what "he's" not saying, "his" blood alcohol level, what's protocol and so on. It seems these past 21 months have been all about "John Doe".

Where is Leisha in all of this? The courts and attorneys deal with this type of issue all the time. They check to be sure the right paperwork is filed, laws are followed, chain of custody established, etc., and with no disrespect intended...I feel become desensitized to the issue at hand. Leisha is NOT a bunch of words in a file. She's NOT just a name within a police report. Leisha was a beautiful, loving, caring, happy 27 year old who had dreams, ambitions and goals. Through all of the paperwork and scheduling, did anyone remember that she's been taken from us???? During the back and forth discussions, legal proceedings and what precedence determines "John Doe's" fate.... Have there been any discussions on Leisha's fate and what SHE and those that love her have lost out on? We had to endure the insensitive statement of how "John Doe" had to hobble out of the hospital that night with no shoes because he hurt his toe. I had to see my daughter in the back room of a funeral home. Her body was cold and so broken, cut and bruised that it didn't even look like the beautiful young woman she'd become. I've not heard anyone discuss the pain she must have felt. Was "she" scared? Was "she" treated fairly?

Leisha had many friends and a very large family that loved her. She'd drop whatever she was doing if someone needed her. She truly was that person that brightened a room just by walking into it...with her smile, her laughter, endless sense of humor and caring nature. The last conversation I had with her was while she was on her way to go out that evening. We were discussing her uncle who had died the day before and how his daughter was so angry. She said, "We're a strong family and always there for each other. We just need to stick together and we'll get through this." No matter how difficult the situation, Leisha would process the pain and frustration then begin looking for a positive way to move forward. The world needs more people like Leisha.

......That's the light and the joy that's been lost.

Leisha had many dreams and wanted to do so many things. She loved adventure. She couldn't get enough of life. She and her sister have always been very close and Ashley has been lost without her. Leish was her best friend. They wanted to be each other's maid of honor at their weddings. They wanted their children to grow up together. That and so much more has been ripped from them....from all of us that loved her. There are no words to describe the loss and the pain and the emptiness we feel with losing Leisha. I'll never get to see her have her own children or buy the home she dreamed of having. She had just finished renovating an old and very dilapidated apartment. She replaced windows and flooring and every inch was painted and brightened. She'd begun making furniture and designing home décor and a line of greeting cards. She couldn't wait to get her own home to put her creative ideas into that home. We talked about that often. I was so proud of her.

Leisha dated "John Doe" a few years ago but she soon realized that he drank and partied too much, was controlling, had anger issues and said he had no direction in life. She told me that she didn't like how he never took accountability for his actions, was insecure and was so jealous. He'd get angry at her if she was talking to one of her male cousins or friends later accusing her of "sleeping with them."

In July, just before her death, she'd broken up from a long-term relationship. "John Doe" immediately began pressuring her to date him. Leisha told him she wasn't ready but he wouldn't back off. At our granddaughter's birthday party – the end of July, "John Doe" showed up and sat in his car out on the street. I asked Leisha what was going on and she told me he was angry about something again but didn't know what. She told me he'd been pressuring her to marry him. She said she told him he hadn't changed and had no intentions to but didn't want to hurt his feelings so was trying to slowly pull away from him.

Video surveillance from one of the bars shows "John Doe" with two drinks in his hands while hitting on another girl that evening. It later shows him leaving the bar with that same girl. There is no communication from him to Leisha for some time according to her phone and what her friends have told us. Then when "John Doe" is done with the other girl, he begins playing controlling games again...with Leisha. According to her phone records as well as statements from two men that Leisha knew and she had been talking with, "John Doe" began calling and texting her obsessively at the end of the night. These two men told me that "John Doe" pulled up in front of "XYZ Pizza" and his car reeked of burning oil and rubber. He began screaming at her to get in the car. He then got out of the car, (please excuse my language...) began yelling loudly at her in front of the crowd, called her an F'n hoar, and other worse names. He got back in the car and screamed at her to get in. Leisha was a pacifist and I'm sure had become used to his angry episodes so I have no doubt she figured this was just one more, so complied. A police officer from" Town O" observed this behavior and saw him flailing his arms at her as she got in the car so began to approach them. "John Doe" sped away.

Minutes later the toll booth worker has given her account of "John Doe" pulling up, asking to use a bathroom and when told "No", he became angry. She could smell the alcohol from the car and observed

Leisha covered with a blanket or towel up over her face and not moving. An email from "John Doe" after the accident states that Leisha didn't have her seat belt on because she was helping get toll money. According to the toll booth worker, she did not. Was she unconscious from him hitting her?? Seconds later Leisha is lying on the tar with multiple injuries.

My daughter who was light, fun and happy...always caring about other people's needs and feelings was treated like dirt by this kid. She had just lost her uncle and instead of treating her well, he showed her disrespect and anger for no reason.

"John Doe's" parents paid thousands of dollars for his bail. He clearly demonstrated a lack of respect not only for them and us by going right out drinking at bars but a clear disrespect for the law as well. Before he was arrested for breaking the bail conditions, he was bragging on Facebook (please excuse my language but to quote him) how he had life by the balls, a new girlfriend and was rebuilding a new car. He also posted a video of himself racing a car. All just a few weeks after Leisha's death...that he caused.

Recently I learned that after the vehicle autopsy, "John Doe" wanted to keep his car, which was totaled, and have it stored at his parent's house. It's another clear indication of his lack of character and a lack of respect for anyone. My daughter lost her life in that car!! Yet he wants to keep it. That tells me he doesn't think he did a thing wrong... that tells me he's not taking accountability for what he did, there's no remorse or guilt! His drinking, his rage, his disrespect for anyone, including the law, took Leisha from us.

Her birthday was 3 weeks ago. She would have been 29. My children define me. They've always been the joy in my life. I can't begin to describe the desperation I feel at times needing to hear her voice, her laughter, share her day or how it feels to have holidays and life without her being part of it. I want to hold her and to see her...but I can't. Some days, it's truly all I can do, just to breathe. I miss my daughter. Everything feels broken without her. She did nothing wrong...cared about his feelings and was taken from us because of his rage, games, irresponsibility and disrespect. None of which I see any evidence that he feels remorseful for.

The judge thanked me before summarizing what had happened, acknowledging the pain suffered by all then provided his judgment against John Doe. Charge 1: Manslaughter. Charge 2: Operating Under the Influence – Death. He was sentenced to eight years in jail with all but thirty-two months suspended and given a four-year probation. His right to drive any automobile was also revoked for life but he can petition this judgment after his probationary period ends. His fourteen months spent in jail while awaiting sentencing was knocked off the final jail time, leaving eighteen months left to serve. We were told he would most likely accrue good behavior time as well as long as he didn't cause trouble while serving his time in jail. I was glad that he received these charges but was very disappointed with what a light sentence was given. John Doe gave an apology but only after months of denial and when finally cornered by evidence. They were empty, monotone words with no sincerity or merit behind them.

When I got into my car, I instantly felt a need to call Leisha, to tell her it was over and she was safe to come home now. I found myself dumbfounded as to where that came from. My mind must have subconsciously moved her to some hidden, protected place where he couldn't hurt her anymore. It really felt as though she had been away and it was time to come home. I was shocked and completely unaware that this delusion had formulated without waking knowledge or intention. Reality hit hard. Putting him in jail didn't bring her back. It did not make it all ok. I felt the loss all over again. Later when listening to the CD our grief counselor had given us, the song, "Too Early in the Morning" was playing. As I listened, some of the words had more depth and finality, "I guess it's finally hit me what forever really means, that no amount of dreaming is gonna bring you back to me."

Struggling through twenty-one months of the civil and criminal legal proceedings has been difficult. The emotional roller coaster of reliving details of Leisha's death, the constant barrage of red tape, documentation errors and scheduling delays are only a few of the challenges that were thrown at us. Each act of negligence or irresponsibility of those playing a role in that evenings events were brought to the table. With each, our feelings were validated just be- fore being told we had no legal recourse. I fought on every level, only to learn how fluffy words mask the injustice of what's called the justice system. Now, with the legalities behind us, I wonder whether the process was worth the added level of frustration. Did forcing the truth lessen our grief or suffering? Did his sentencing compensate for the pain inflicted on Leish or any of us? Did it bring her back to us? No.

That evening when I got into bed, I was heavy with emotion and emptiness. I saw a large circle of pink energy appear. I then received a vision of Jesus wearing the crown of thorns. It took me a long time to understand why he showed himself to me this way. When Jesus proclaimed he was the son of God, he was tortured and a crown of thorns was placed on his head in mockery before being nailed to a cross. His suffering and sacrifice, was met with victory though. He conquered death. He is the Messiah, Lord of all...a true king who now wears a crown of gold. We too can be subjected to injustice, pain and suffering. Leisha suffered and right now it feels like justice was not served. But Jesus will one day provide the true judgement, one that *is* just.

Romans 12:19 NIV

Do not take revenge, my dear friends, but leave room for God's wrath, for it is written: "It is mine to avenge; I will repay, says the Lord.

May 18, 2012: I was lying in bed with the lights off just thinking of the day's events. A blue tinted light flowing into my room appeared. It was on a horizontal angle and coming in from the window area towards my bed. I then saw various colored energies appear brightly at the end of my bed. Body shapes took form. The blue light was narrow towards the back, by the window, and wider at the foot of my bed where they both stood. I feel that one was Leisha and one was my Dad. There were other people behind them but I don't know who they were.

May 20, 2012: While writing about the sentencing, I kept seeing red and black energy flash around me. I could see other colored energy too. Worrying that the other colored energy was Leisha, I told her that I was ok and to stay away from the bad energies. I told her to stay safe. Seconds after saying these words to Leisha, a vision of God's hands holding Leisha in the middle of them appeared to me. She was tiny in his large, strong, protective hands. She is safe. We are protected. Thank you, God.

Chapter

Eleven

✺

All Things Do Work Together
For Good

*It takes pain to see peace, loss to see gain
and anger to feel love.*

June 4, 2012: I saw an angel standing in my bedroom today. Her arms were by her side and I could see the tips of her wings down below her hands. Her hair hung behind her shoulders so I couldn't see how long it was. The first time I saw her, she was a distance away. The second time, she was right next to my bed. When redrawing the original sketch I'd made when first seeing this angel, I couldn't get it quite right. Every time I'd finish up a drawing, it didn't look the way I had remembered her. Just before starting the fifth attempt, I closed my eyes trying to remember exactly how had she had appeared to me. As I did, she appeared again but this time showed me only the corner of her face and one of her eyes. Blue twinkles were speckled about her face and hair. She was providing validation for me that the twinkles I see are angels. One particular angel that I see sometimes has such brilliant, crystally, blue twinkles. I believe they're hers.

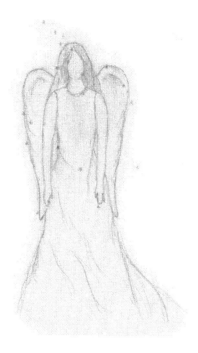

June 22, 2012: While at work, I had met with a co-worker to show her some of my drawings. After chatting for a few minutes, she told me how her daughter had changed careers and became a nurse. Shortly after, a traffic accident occurred outside a convenience store she had just stopped at. Had she not moved into the medical profession, she wouldn't have known how to help a man that was severely injured in that accident. Because she did, she was able to save this man's life. When returning to my office, I was thinking about how God guides us with His Holy Spirit. I was feeling so blessed to be given the gift of visions and for Jesus and God to open my heart to them. While sitting at my desk thinking of these things, a sudden large flash of gold and white light appeared in the corner of my office. I heard a slight electrical sound at the same time. At first I thought my laptop or monitor was shorting out but there wasn't any smoke and it continued to work without issues. I then realized I had been visited by an angel. Archangel Gabriel is said to have colors of gold and white and brings us blessing of protection, intuition, clarity and discipline. I have no proof of this but whether it was him or another angel, I feel blessed to have had their presence near.

July 19, 2012: Blue twinkles appeared in front of me tonight, spreading about three feet long and ten inches deep. Within seconds, on my right I saw an angel with auburn hair, wavy and perfectly combed. Behind her, I saw tall wings that extended upright as if landing from flight. Then...I saw her nose. It was Leisha's nose!! She was showing me her nose because she always thought it was too big and I always told her how beautiful she was and that I thought she had a cute turned up nose. She wanted me to see her nose and hair so I would know it was her! I see other angels and some have long hair like hers but I never see their facial features so wonder at times if it's Leisha. My heart leapt and I called out her name in excitement! Then I saw her arms stretched out over me. I'm not sure if that was to tell me she's watching over me? Then her hands moved in and were cupped together and filled with very bright light. Seconds later, she showed me her dress. It was long, had blue tones and varying layers at the bottom. A few more seconds and she showed me a large butterfly. It was about 3 feet high with the shape and design just like the small silver one I have at work leaning against her picture, except this one was much larger and beautifully colored with blues and areas of green and fuchsia. The colors glimmered. Beautiful!! She knows that butterflies remind me of her. They represent transformation, plus one of the last videos we have of her, she and Lexy were chasing a butterfly in our back yard. You can hear Leisha's voice say, "But-ter-*fly*" then giggle when Lexy ran after it. While living on earth, our souls are contained within our bodies...like a cocoon. Leisha's soul was released with beautiful wings taking flight.

2 Corinthians 5:6-8 NIV

"Therefore we are always confident and know that as long as we are at home in the body we are away from the Lord. For we live by faith, not by sight. We are confident, I say, and would prefer to be away from

the body and at home with the Lord."

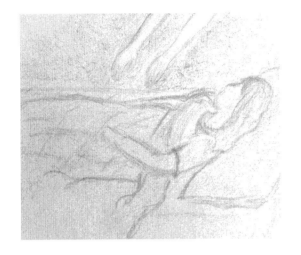

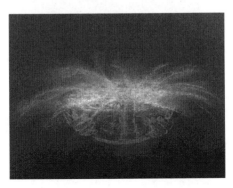

Several weeks ago, Ashley and Lexy were driving in their car.

Lexy exclaimed, "Mommy look! It's Ya Ya up in the sky!!" "You see Ya Ya, Lexy?!" my daughter asked. "Yes! On that cloud!" "What is she wearing?" Ashley asked. A blue Tinker Bell dress." With Lexy being just shy of 4 years old and watching a lot of children's movies, I thought she might have "embellished" a bit when describing Leisha's dress. Leish wanted me to know she in fact did have a blue Tinker Bell shaped dress on when she appeared to Lexy. I drew the above picture of Leisha wearing the dress she had shown me. When I showed it to Lexy and asked who this was. Without missing a beat, she said, "That's Ya Ya with her wings."

Leisha is safe...she's good...she still exists...just as Jesus promised. To see her and know that she's with God and Jesus brings such comfort and peace. No matter how I've described the devastation we've felt throughout this book, I've not been able to find the sufficient words to adequately portray any of it. I was shattered in so many ways when I lost her. My soul was emptied. The pain has been overwhelming but Jesus has been there the whole time, showing me love, guiding me and bringing comfort. He showed me that Leisha lives on within a beautiful world that awaits us when our physical lives end. I'm so, so grateful.

My cousin Tom's health has been declining rapidly over the last few months. A planned family reunion was moved to an earlier date so that he could attend. Today, my Mom, daughter and granddaughter and I set off sharing a long ride to the family gathering. Four generations spending the day together was fun. It was wonderful talking with family members that I hadn't seen for quite some time. Tom was able to attend and enjoyed himself. Everyone spent quality time with him, taking lots of pictures. He was in good spirits despite how tired and ill he was. Tom has always been such a happy, loving and caring man. He served in the armed forces in his younger years. Later in life, he was a member of the Shriner's serving in many ways, one of which was a performing as a clown for the Shriner's circus. Tom was always laughing and joking. I don't remember him as anything other than kind. Despite the sadness of his failing health, it was wonderful to spend time with him and our family members for the day.

July 21, 2012: I woke early in the morning and was just lying in bed thinking about this or that, wondering what the day would bring. A vision of my cousin Tom suddenly filled my view. He was walking (from my right to left) and looking slightly upward. He stopped, turning to his left to briefly look at me before turning back and continuing onward. I was then shown the number "5". The spiritual meaning of the number 5 is travel and motion. I anxiously waited for a few hours to pass before calling his home to see how he was doing. His daughter told me that he'd had a horrible night. She said he cried out to God over and over to take him because the pain was so unbearable. God answered him. His soul was released. I saw him ascend to heaven before his body stopped working!! He no longer looked sick with cancer but healthy as he did before his illness. Four days later, Tom's physical body gave in. This vision provided proof that God can take our souls when we're suffering whether from pain due to sickness, an accident or violence, even before physical death. He's watching over all of us, at every moment. The gift I was just given brings such relief. I often agonize about how much pain Leisha may have felt during that horrible accident. I now feel confident that He took her before she felt any pain.

October 15, 2012: I dreamed I was with a man who had cleared trees and smaller brush out from around a barn. I looked up to see the lower branches of oak trees that had been pruned leaving a full canopy of branches with bright green leaves at the top. Those that were left just below the canopy had been trimmed back close to the trunk, leaving stubs of about 3-4 feet long. On the way to work the next morning, the message being told on the morning radio program included "pruning of the vines." The next evening, for a change, I wanted to read in the New Testament instead of the old. Randomly flipping it open, it landed on John 15:

John 15:1-17 NIV
"I am the true vine, and my Father is the gardener. He cuts off every branch in me that bears no fruit, while every branch that does bear fruit he prunes so that it will be even more fruitful. You are already clean because of the word I have spoken to you. Remain in me, as I also remain in you. No branch can bear fruit by itself; it must remain in the vine. Neither can you bear fruit unless you remain in me." "I am the vine; you are the branches. If you remain in me and I in you, you will bear much fruit; apart from me you can do nothing. If you do not remain in me, you are like a branch that is thrown away and withers; such branches are picked up, thrown into the fire and burned. If you remain in me and my words remain in you, ask whatever you wish, and it will be done for you. This is to my Father's glory, that you bear much fruit, showing yourselves to be my disciples."

"As the Father has loved me, so have I loved you. Now remain in my love. If you keep my commands, you will remain in my love, just as I have kept my Father's commands and remain in his love. I have told you this so that my joy may be in you and that your joy may be complete. My command is this: Love each other as I have loved you.

Greater love has no one than this: to lay down one's life for one's friends. You are my friends if you do what I command. I no longer call you servants, because a servant does not know his master's business. In- stead, I have called you friends, for everything that I learned from my Father I have made known to you. You did not choose me, but I chose you and appointed you so that you might go and bear fruit—fruit that will last—and so that whatever you ask in my name the Father will give you. This is my command: Love each other."

This was another message gently placed in my path. As with all the others, it was my choice whether I take notice and embraced it. Each message has led me to the next, each giving me a better understanding and in turn a need to know more. I'm a gardener and spend a lot of time pruning and feeding my plants so that they're strong and produce abundant flowers or vegetables. This passage is the same concept except it applies to our lives. God and Jesus are our nourishment and caretakers. Without them, we eventually wither away and die.

I received a letter from the State of Maine Department of Corrections, notifying us that John Doe had requested furlough, which is an "authorized leave without official escort granted to a prisoner from a correctional facility." The letter stated that we had an opportunity to provide our opinions on whether he should have this request granted. Leisha's Dad and I both submitted statements disagreeing. We heard nothing more until in May, when another letter was received. This one was notifying us that he would be released from jail in June 2013, having completed his incarceration. I called the correctional facility to inquire why he was being released so early. His end date should have been around November of 2013.

The Director of Victim Services told me that he had accrued good behavior time which allowed him early release. When asking how he accrued this time, I was told that he'd been participating in a work release program, where he could leave the correctional facility each day to work at a public job. He'd also participated in substance abuse counseling. All of this allowed a reduction in his sentence of approximately six months. She also told me that he'd been allowed to go visit his parents for three days in April of 2013, which we had no idea had been approved. Apparently, our statements had no influence or consideration. I couldn't believe it. He got three days off to visit his parents and got to leave each day for work. I felt like the whole legal process was just for show. They couldn't even make him serve the full eighteen months behind locked doors for driving enraged, drunk and recklessly enough to take someone's life...my daughter's life. On top of that, while there, he got to leave each day for work and leave to visit his family. How is any of that punishment?? Maine officials boast about their tough drunk driving laws but I've seen no evidence of them.

The message of Jesus being the vine and abiding in him was good timing. Receiving the information about John Doe's release from jail left me feeling frustrated. Leisha is gone and all he seemed to get was a slap on the wrist. The anger that fueled me during those months of fighting for justice only brought more frustration and pain. I've learned that I can't make things whole again nor can "I" bring back the peace I once held. While buried under layers of pain and destruction, messages were being provided to help me find my way. Jesus helped me see that peace can only be found in Him. I couldn't do it on my own. He showed me that I have a choice. I can continue living life my way or I can choose to be connected in Him.

His truth is all we need. He protects us from any force, any devastation, any obstacle. It doesn't mean that I forget all that's happened. It means that I can let go. I can place it in His hands and find peace.

A very close friend, Elise, has been by my side throughout this hardship. She's one of the most spiritual, compassionate and positive people I know. It's been good to have her as a sounding board and support. She's asked me to see if any messages might be provided to her through my visions. I'd declined several times but one evening, she convinced me to try. After saying a prayer, I closed my eyes to meditate. A white horse instantly appeared and it was if I was riding on his back. We traveled through a vast open plain made up of what looked like billions of micro sized, blue, purple and greenish colored clear beads that glimmered with their own elements of light and space. Then a white, middle aged gentleman appeared before me. He was holding a two or three-year old little girl up in the air. A moment later, he was giving that same girl a piggy back ride but she now appeared to be about five or six years old. Next, he was sitting and an angel appeared behind him. Purity and light radiated from every bit of her being. Even her hair emanated brightness from within. She reached around to his chest and pulled it open, revealing his lungs. There was no blood or goriness with this gesture, just a revealing of his lungs. She then began circling her hands, one clockwise and the other counter clockwise, in front of his lungs. As I was describing this to Elise, it came to me what they were trying to tell me. I said to her, "Didn't your Dad die of lung disease?!" As she confirmed, I saw the man reach out his hand towards me in greeting. Elise's Dad was very ill when I first met her so I never had the opportunity to meet him...until today. I also felt

134

incredibly honored to be granted this message to relay to my dear friend. She used to tell me how hard it was to watch her Dad struggling to breathe. He and this amazingly, glorious angel wanted her to know he was watched over, comforted and healed. People are healed of their injuries and illnesses when they pass into God's kingdom!! I was blessed with another beautiful message today. I want to share with as many people as I can in hopes that it brings them as much comfort as it did me, knowing my Leisha was healed also.

In August of 2011, I'd had a vision of three angels on top of what looked like clouds. They appeared to be watching over some sort of opening in the cloud, which appeared to be a gateway or entrance of some sort. It was a closed in, circular shaped hole but the color and shading were different, defining it from the rest of the clouded area. I had done a quick sketch at the time and now wanted to finalize the drawing to add to my book but couldn't remember some of the details. While working on it, I kept asking the angels to help me remember exactly what they looked like. Did all three have long hair? What did their clothing look like? Did their clothing have sleeves? Were their wings up or down? I worked on it for a couple of hours or so before deciding it reflected as best as it could, the vision I had been shown. Later in the day, I decided to take a few minutes to meditate. After just a minute or two, a beautiful pure white horse appeared to me. This is the only horse I've seen that has wings and has come to me now on a few occasions. (Though I don't know what gender he truly is, I'm referring to him as male.) He came straight at me, turned to one side then circled around me stopping on the other side. I then noticed the back of his neck and was looking straight down at his white mane. I remember thinking to myself, "Wow, it's as if I'm riding on his back." No sooner had that thought crossed my mind when I realized I had been on a journey, which had now ended in just a few short moments. There before me were the three angels I had been trying to draw. One by one, each showed me their clothing, hair and exact positions they had been in months earlier when I had the vision. I watched in amazement, filled with joy and awe as I realized what was happening. This was yet another confirmation that I was being called upon by God and Jesus to write this book, share my experiences so that others will know of His Grace and love. My phone suddenly rang which distracted me. I kept trying to focus but the clarity slowly faded. I ignored my phone and quickly sketched what I had just seen on a scrap piece of paper, redrawing them in my sketch book the next evening. I feel so honored to be blessed with such a special gift. The words holiness and magnificence come to mind but seem so inadequate to describe such awesome beauty and glory.

November 2, 2012: While lying in bed that evening, I saw blue and fuchsia energy appear. I then saw a crowd of people gathered together. My focus went to one person in the center of the crowd. His head was thrown back, his mouth wide open, screaming in pain and agony. My heart filled with sorrow. Were these lost souls? Silently within my mind, I cried out to them, "Go to Jesus! He died as a sacrifice for all our sins. Believe in him and all that he is. Accept him as your savior. He's waiting for you." A cross then appeared to me. I continued, "He just showed me the cross, telling me that he forgives you. I see the angels! They're all waiting for you. Don't let Satan or his minions trick you. Don't listen to their lies! They can't hurt you if you don't let them. Believe in Jesus, his sacrifice and love. The promise of heaven is real! Jesus is waiting for you. Peace, warmth and happiness are yours. You can be free from your pain! Go to him!" As I was desperately looking for the right words to reach their hearts, I saw several souls go to Christ. He held them in his arms, one by one. The rest remained in the darkness as my vision faded. I was amazed at what I'd just seen! I then realized that I was in that "dark place" and wasn't afraid. I could only think of telling them all about Jesus, of his word, of his grace, his promise. Did I say enough? Did I say the right things? Why didn't all of them go to Him? After writing the above, it was dinner time so decided to stop and put my notes away for the evening. I'd had my bible next to me for reference so closed it and headed to my bedroom. As I placed it down, I randomly flipped it open, which landed on John 14:

John 14 NIV

"Do not let your hearts be troubled. You believe in God; believe also in me. My Father's house has many rooms; if that were not so, would I have told you that I am going there to prepare a place for you? And if I go and prepare a place for you, I will come back and take you to be

with me that you also may be where I am. You know the way to the place where I am going."

Thomas said to him, "Lord, we don't know where you are going, so how can we know the way?"

Jesus answered, "I am the way and the truth and the life. No one comes to the Father except through me. If you really know me, you will know my Father as well. From now on, you do know him and have seen him."

The only way to God and His kingdom is by believing that Jesus is the true son of God and that he died on the cross for our sins. His blood was shed for us. Some of the souls I saw must not have accepted this because they didn't go to Him. It gives me such comfort and joy to know that others did! It validates to me that God's word is true and the *only* truth. My heart is bursting with awe and gratitude.

On July 23, 2012, I had a vision of many people walking in a long line which was four to five people deep and they were standing side by side. I couldn't see an end to the line it was so long. Usually when I see people in a line, it's only one person standing behind another and they're coming towards me. This time they were walking from right to left and slightly upward. I spoke to them with my thoughts, silently asking where they were going but received no response. I looked ahead to the beginning of the line of people hoping to gain an understanding of what they were all doing. As I watched, the underside of a cloud suddenly appeared. Just as I noticed the cloud I physically heard, like it was right in the room next to me, what sounded like an electrical wire shorting out!! The cloud snapped open revealing blue skies above. All the souls were migrating towards this opening. Heaven!!! Each and every one was being granted entry into the promise land. No wonder no one acknowledged me when I called to them, they were entering God's kingdom! Shortly after losing Leisha, I was shown the vision of three angels watching over a closed in circle on top of the clouds. At the time, I wondered if it were a "door" or entry of some sort into heaven. This vision now validates that my assumptions were correct. I wonder and marvel at what it will be like to be greeted with love by our loved ones, the angels, our Lord Jesus and God as we enter into heaven. I can't help but smile as I think of it all.

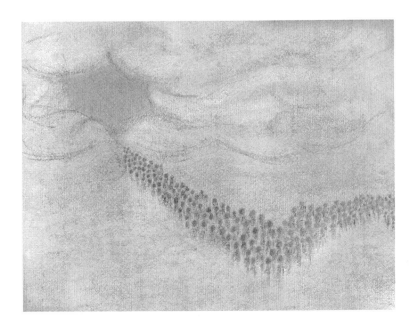

Quite some time later, I was provided a vision of a book. There were no other objects in the vision, just a book with the words, "The Silver Cord" written on it. No pictures on the cover, just those words. I thought that I was being shown a book that I should read so began researching a book with that title. I was unable to find one but did find a reference to Ecclesiastes which reads:

Ecclesiastes 12:6-7 NIV

"Remember him—before the silver cord is severed, and the golden bowl is broken; before the pitcher is shattered at the spring, and the wheel broken at the well, and the dust returns to the ground it came from, and the spirit returns to God who gave it."

While researching the meaning of this scripture, I found that chapter 12 focuses on the life and death of a man. It's thought that the golden bowl represents his head, the pitcher and the wheel represent his heart and ability to circulate blood through his body.

All three represent his physical decline. Once they are broken, our bodies return to the ground as dust and our souls return to God who gave it. The silver cord is a life thread connecting our soul to our physical body. It separates when we die, leaving an empty shell behind. This passage is reminding us to live our lives in God while we're here on earth because it will be too late once we die and the silver cord is severed. We should also look to God while we're young because it can be hard to find Him when we're old and facing physical and mental decline.

Not long after that vision, I received another one of a man running and crying out. A long thin ribbon or cord like object was attached and trailing behind him. Both he and the cord were whitish in color yet kind of translucent. He was a distance away at first, running from right to left before turning and coming towards me. He stopped just to my right and looked up. His face expressed pain or anguish. Just as I had noticed his expression, Jesus appeared. I then saw Jesus and the man ascend upwards. My next vision of them was seeing them walking away, side by side. Jesus was leading him by the hand and between their hands was a ball of white light. That light was his soul, his silver cord! It all came together. I had been

shown the book title, "Silver Cord", so that I could research and be prepared for this vision. How wonderful to be given this additional validation that when our physical bodies stop working, our soul (our silver cord) departs and Jesus is there waiting to receive it. Emotion and awe flood through me as I think of the gift He offers all of us. Open your heart to Jesus! Accept his love and sacrifice made for you! He is there waiting for all who believe. Imagine what it will be like to feel His hand in ours, to feel our soul in His care. I think back to when Leisha showed me the light in her hands. She was trying to show me her soul, that she lives on. It's comforting and so beautifully overwhelming!

Many months later, while at church one morning, the pastor asked us to bow our heads for prayer time. The moment I did a new message was revealed to me. It was as if I were standing at the back of the church and slightly above everyone looking down upon them. They were all sitting just as they were at that moment but above their head's I could see wavy lines ascending upwards. As with many of my visions, a knowing is there like someone is whispering to me. I instantly knew that the wavy lines were their prayers!! I could see them drifting upwards towards God. The bible is filled with passages that teach us about prayer. As a flesh and blood man Jesus used prayer, which shows us that He needed God just as we do. If the son of God used prayer, how much more validity do we need to show its value? Envisioning Jesus praying suddenly silences the noise in life around me. It's as if only the two of them exist. It's the same for each one of us. God is omniscient which means he gives each of us His undivided attention. The song, "What a Friend We Have in Jesus" summarizes it so well. It's a song I've heard many times but had never contemplated the words before. I especially like the second verse.

What a Friend we have in Jesus,
All our sins and griefs to bear
What a privilege to carry
Everything to God in prayer

O what peace we often forfeit,
O what needless pain we bear,
All because we do not carry

Everything to God in prayer

What a beautiful gift to be allowed this vision!! God wants us to know that no matter who we are, we can go to Him in prayer. He hears each, and every one of us.

Philippians 4:6 NIV
"Do not be anxious about anything, but in every situation, by prayer and petition, with thanksgiving, present your requests to God."

Psalm 55:22 NIV
"Cast your cares on the Lord and he will sustain you. He will never let the righteous be shaken."

Proverbs 3:6 NIV
"In all your ways submit to Him, and He will make your paths straight."

.... According to God,

Deuteronomy 30:15-20 NIV

"See, I set before you today life and prosperity, death and destruction. For I command you today to love the Lord your God, to walk in obedience to him, and to keep his commands, decrees and laws; then you will live and increase, and the Lord your God will bless you in the land you are entering to possess."

"But if your heart turns away and you are not obedient, and if you are drawn away to bow down to other gods and worship them, I declare to you this day that you will certainly be destroyed. You will not live long in the land you are crossing the Jordan to enter and possess."

"This day I call the heavens and the earth as witnesses against you that I have set before you life and death, blessings and curses. Now choose life, so that you and your children may live and that you may love the Lord your God, listen to his voice, and hold fast to him. For the Lord is your life, and he will give you many years in the land he swore to give to your fathers, Abraham, Isaac and Jacob."

Matthew 7:24-27 NIV
"Therefore everyone who hears these words of mine and puts them into practice is like a wise man who built his house on the rock. The rain came down, the streams rose, and the winds blew and beat against that house; yet it did not fall, because it had its foundation on the rock. But everyone who hears these words of mine and does not put them into practice is like a foolish man who built his house on the sand. The rain came down, the streams rose, and the winds blew and beat against that house, and it fell with a great crash."

.... According to Leisha,

Excerpt from Leisha's diary, just one year before the accident, regarding a time she'd been dating a man who owned a Harley David- son motorcycle:

8/23/09: " I enjoy long rides, especially when there are farms, barns, fields and old country stores to gaze upon. As we ride, these things are part of our journey and I day dream, as always, of what it would be like to have my own house. ...someday."

"We run into some people he had met one other time. Troy and Tina. Nice people. We took a walk with them through what seemed to be a

small village. Buildings seemed short which made me feel large, especially with my 4 inch heels on. We climbed sets of stairs, which brought us to a roof top café. We sat at the bar with Troy and Tina and sipped Sangria. I felt so comfortable. It was such a perfect spot to have drinks and even though the sun wasn't shining, it felt just as good to be embraced by the fog. The combination of being on a roof top and my head blanketed by the clouds made me feel like I was soaring in the sky. Very free and happy. Maybe this is why the birds sing their songs."

Excerpt from Leisha's diary... This was written in her diary just a couple of months before the accident.

Spring of 2010: "May what you see in the mirror delight you, and what others see in you delight them. May someone love you enough to forgive your faults, be blind to your blemishes and tell the world about your virtues. May you remember to say "I love you" at least once a day to your spouse, child, parents and siblings. May we live in a world of awareness and love... in every sunset, every flower's unfolding petals, every baby's smile, every lover's kiss... and every wonderful astonishing, miraculous beat of our hearts."

The Beginning

Epilogue

I've had a gift of visions all my life. Looking back, I feel that I was being tested through the years to see what purpose I would use it for. I now see and fully believe that all things are by, for and under God and God only. It's our choice on how the gifts are used and who they serve. I must have passed the tests because when we lost Leisha, that gift became much stronger. God allowed me to see and learn through my journey so that I could share this story with others, using it for His...and our...greater good. We're visual people and we often need validation and proof to accept truths. He's allowed that through me so that I can share with others in hopes that they too can believe. The world is becoming more and more challenging to live in. Now more than ever, we need a reminder of His grace and refuge.

When Leisha was taken from us, my life shattered into a million pieces. I was broken, lost and angry. I cursed God for not protecting my daughter, yet he returned only love. When my mind and body were aching with pain, grief and exhaustion, he sent an angel whose physical touch brought relief and comfort. When I was con- fused, and seeking guidance and knowledge, he provided visions and words that just happen to be spoken that day on the radio or a movie helping me understand something I had questioned. My journey has been a difficult and painful one but Jesus guided me through. He carried me when I needed it. He enlightened my mind and heart with knowledge and understanding. He's brought peace back to my soul. I have peace in knowing my daughter still exists and that we will be together again someday. I also have peace in coming to know Him and all that He is and has done for us.

I had built a foundation based on my own principles and beliefs. Though it was a solid and loving foundation, it wasn't strong enough to support the level of tragedy that came into my life. I was totally and utterly lost. The initial visions halted my decent and sparked hope but it remained a difficult uphill battle. The pain and anger that I harbored within allowed darkness to find its way to me. Evil beings used my pain and need to see Leisha, to discourage and trick me. I could have very easily given in to it but Jesus and the angels were patient, loving and protecting. They never left my side. They allowed time for me to learn and grow while I was healing and dredging through the legal proceedings and the medical issues my other daughter was facing. I was provided continuous messages and visions to help me find the right path. During that process, I thought by telling souls to "go into the light" that they would automatically find their way to heaven. I thought that by telling bad souls that I was protected by the blood of Jesus, they would leave me alone. It didn't work because they were still just words. It took time for all of it to resonate because my mind and heart were so clouded. The more I opened myself to Jesus though and the more I studied His word, the more my faith grew. Without realizing it, that faith was subtly and silently weaving a garment of protection. One day, when re-reading the words, "If God is for me, who can be against me?" they seem to leap off the page with such power. I finally "saw". It was at that moment when I realized that I was wearing the full armor of God. It was also at that moment when all negative forces went... and stayed away. I stand now on a new foundation. One that I have literally tested and tried. Nothing can shake it because it is of God.

We face so many challenges in today's world. Terrorism, abuse and murder are becoming more prevalent. People endure terminal illnesses, addictions and other medical constraints. Medical costs are rising out of control yet insurance coverage is decreasing. No matter the challenge or tragedy, we all suffer and we all feel pain. More than ever, we need faith in God. His word is our compass. It points the way to peace and comfort. Whether consumed with grief from losing a loved one, facing illness, job loss or whatever it may be, we're all in God's hands. Whether you've built that foundation before or after a tragedy strikes, He's always there. Had I known God and Jesus before losing Leisha, the level of devastation would have been so much less. Another area that would have been easier to get through was that of the EMT and police officer that seemed to have fallen short. I wanted to punish anyone that hurt or didn't protect her. Seeking restitution didn't provide the relief that I thought it would. It only added to the anguish I was already suffering. I was too filled with grief and anger to see anything other than incompetence. With that level of pain and grief removed, I now see how so many public servants risk their own lives to save others. Had my faith and knowledge of God's word been in place, I wouldn't have suffered such anger and retaliation.

When our time on earth ends, there's a kingdom waiting for us. It's where my daughter now resides peacefully and safely. We're healed when passing from this physical world into the spiritual one. In heaven, there are no more barriers of age, pain, injury or illness. There's no more grief and no more tears. God is, was and is to come. Jesus *is* the son of God. He lived among us and died as a sacrifice for all of us. Believe in Him and you will have eternal life in the kingdom of God. He's there waiting to greet and heal us.

John 3:16 NIV
"For God so loved the world that he gave His one and only Son, that whoever believes in Him shall not perish but have eternal life."

1 Corinthians 15:20-21 NIV
"But Christ has indeed been raised from the dead, the first fruits of those who have fallen asleep. For since death came through a man the resurrection of the dead comes also through a man."

Revelation 21:4
"He will wipe every tear from their eyes. There will be no more death or mourning or crying or pain, for the old order of things has passed away."

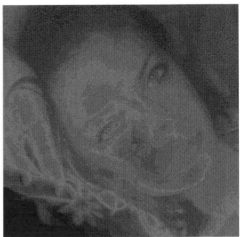

Made in the USA
Middletown, DE
13 June 2019